Copyright © 20

No part of this publication may be reproduced, distributed, or transmitted in any form or by any means, including photocopying, recording, or other electronic or mechanical methods, without the prior written permission of the author and publisher, except in the case of brief quotations embodied in reviews and certain other non-commercial uses permitted by copyright law.

Unauthorized reproduction or distribution of this copyrighted work is illegal.

Cover Design: Ashley J. Gallaher-Pollard

Ω
veins of pluto

veins of pluto, solidifying plum ichor in my trenches
sustaining the assemblage of the dark ilk.
emollient lilac, your fetching fragrance clings
to all the pages in the sanctuary, eternal garden within leather leaves.
the fingerprints of my slanted handwriting are supposed to tell a story
in its curves, dips, and shanks,
but that is a memoir that should only be deciphered;
a puzzle of the soul, and the prize is terrible —
instead, see the immaculate chaos of dreams become corporeal
where your name is a word of power
imbued with ancestral prowess and the blessings of Them,
an opulent palimpsest, each one more intricate and excruciating than the last.

and that is what it is like, when I create.

she sells seashells

she sells seashells by the seashore,
but I peddle pride from my front door.
and when they come to try me,
as they always do,
they'll find only magic
and her demon breaking through.

a tender science

and my best nights are begun with the darkest of thoughts
rending, carving, trekking through my heart
cracked throat and torn lips
no, I will sing my songs until they want for nothing
and I will bare my teeth until they grab onto something

every thought poured into the funnel
that sits listless in the well of my void
will spring forth and come to life—
they are not devils and angels
but monsters of my creation;

monsters are taken for evil,
but what is more evil
than the excuse of ignorance?
but is it ignorance if you never knew to ask in the first place?

Ω
my doctor

you are bone melting—
cell reviving, courage inspiring.
you are time; endless
adventure, continuous
trouble ensnared,
mischief? managed.
you are the weathered traveler—
s c o r c h i n g worn
icy knowledge,
wars delivered.
you are perfunctory happiness—
inverted sadness.
you are light in our dark,
love in spite;
carry hope over death.
planet-shattering eyes
star-snaring hearts
nebula fingertips
with a blackhole-sinking smirk.
you came when we needed you
when my galaxy was afloat
savior of my f a t e
gifting spontaneity to me
when the world was making me
old.
Doctor, my Doctor—
you will never be alone.
not even when
the sun is old and grown.
I want you safe, from those false Gods.
you will be thought of,
remembered,
and when it comes time –

saved.

merely guidelines

describe for me the instance in which
you knew you were human:

the day you learned what hate
does to a man, what love does
in return.

the day you learned that life
is not equal, that warriors could not
turn the tides.

the day you bled, shed tears
hot and quick, the bandages that
didn't quite work.

the day you walked out and
were lost, the stranger that pointed
you home.

describe for me the instance in which
you forgot what it means to be human.

Ω
feasting on folly

sumptuous feasts offered on tables of elm,
whilst maple waves extract themselves
from window panes;
'tis the season of magicks deep.

from the frosted edges hunts
the seven devils from paradise
crooning symphonies concocted
for her ears only.

inured against their trappings,
instead, she plays them a song
borne upon the bloodied strings
of dawn and dusk and the last
of her resources.

she is human tonight,
the last thought before the hunted
becomes the hunter;
for the greatest demon
is not the candlelight;
but her.

Ω
the witch and her gunslinger

fifteen years of dirt and dust,
of summoning circles and crop crystals
a bar fight, or nine—
there's always a wager against us,
dry eyes avoiding the truths.
roulette stacks the pot, it grows higher
oh, now a revolver— nobody likes a liar.

but we've got the queen of hearts,
gunslinger.

and we still have the ace of spades,
witch.

do they know what high noon is to a witch?
do they know what a full moon is to a cowboy?

fate isn't written in stone,
I say we write our own.
is that why they don't come 'round?
you think this old woman is going to allow wolves
to prowl my home?
married for a reason!
no sheep live under our roof—
so it is written,
so it will be.

retrouvailles

apricot skies waiting to powder
the world with rainy fingers,
but we have a few moments—

the windows below our feet
catch the end of the day rays,
umbrellas waiting for us at home,
as useful as a needle in
a balloon;

but today is like our companionship:

we are not fair-weather acquaintances,
but forecaster friends,
ready for the rain and wind,
blanket over our shoulders and
latte in our hands,
but embracing the sun when she appears
full smiles and terrible humour,
and perhaps a little sunblock.

smoking ropes

crowds of mongers were
peddling rage and theories
as amelia was led up the stairs,
the hangman waiting to
take her last.

spurs tinkled faintly
the creak of a leather belt,
sharp eyes peered out over
the faces of those that
would eat her alive.

any last words? was the
jeer from her jailer, but
amelia spat at his feet
and the crowds called for
blood;

a twist and jerk secured
her neck at a jaunty angle,
but it was the jailer who
screamed for mercy—

blood-lust turned to
bloody horror, and amelia
slid her noose off while
the man behind her choked
on his own words.

witch! was the cry, and
she touched a finger to
her lips—

careful what you scream for.

Ω
easily disguised

a queasy sensation eggs my limbs into shuddering
left anointed by the sweat that pools in my chest
and reminds me of the anvil that sits there;
heavy-limbed and hard of hearing, there must be something
that will carve away the diseased edges of this anxiety,
left rumbling in the crevasses of nothing.
shaken and chased to the ends of the underworld,
where there was no shelter, it willed itself into being.
and so, I too must be the underworld:
a willful being, creator of sanctuaries that only some will see
are meant to be
a bigger part
of me.

Ω
under the branches of old

long lost wanderer
falling asleep under branches so old
your feet are worn
your heart so heavy,
the theme of your mind, so overwhelming
casting longing glances o'er
the hills of your home;
ne'er to return.
oh, once you may have been proud
a love returned, and hearth of your own
but strife has left you broken
with nowhere left to turn,
and so you call the branches of old
your house and hold…

canada's autumnal magic

welcome home, the Earth says
as the equinox draws closer
the autumn is bountiful;
like sliding into a hot spring
after the hectic summer.
there is always magic in the air
when September brings its colors forth,
waving its flag proudly, cheers erupting joyously.
we change over to hold the trees closer
together, waters cold and sparkling like mercury
bursts of fragrance lingering every day;
oh, what wonders await us,
hidden in the soil, succulent in history.
the autumn is meant for tender mystery,
rapturous renewal and empowered passion.
nothing but good can come from the
richness that fills your lungs
when the leaves turn and the skies glow
like jack-o'-lanterns and church candles.
how does one describe the lush sensation
of starting anew, with the mountains soaring
the trees crooning, the rivers gamboling,
and our hearts braving?
autumn often reminds me that my home
is wherever the mountains are,
when the harvest moon paints its peaks
with the succulent strokes, reminiscent
of van Gogh's brilliant mind.

_____ Ω _____
the world is a paragon

the story always ends at the carfax,
lost in translation, somewhere in the barathrum of the world
like dragon tongues, blundering in the darkness
waiting for purity to light them aflame once more;
diaglyphs lay scattered on my chamber floor,
scented with the oils of lilies and mountain waters
depicting the emergence of all life, scrawled in gold and jewels —
patrons always seemed to discard the thought of nature
and her intimate beauty that surrounds us every day:
what need is there for gold when the rosy light of the sun
soaks the plains more thoroughly than the monsoon rains,
and what use for jewels is there if we have stars,
scintillating and luminous in their navy cradle of velvet,
selcouth but always present in the eyes of those
who can lay claim to the ambitious ideas of the universe?
one day, we will open our eyes as a whole,
and see that the gods never abandoned us —
they were right here before us all along.

Ω
quartermain

the plains of africa whisper and rustle
shaking out the ancestors in the fields
elder magic rising from the dust and dirt
"you shall never —"

tell us, draco, where do we turn
where will be go
without your guidance?
your presence was one of extraordinary measures
as graceful as dragon's flight,
fueled by a long-burning fire —

but you would smile,
that twinkle in your eye that meets mine
and you'd nod your head up.

"to the stars, lass. we've all the time in the world."

written in memory of Sir Sean Connery

―――― Ω ――――
inquisitorial march

by the flames of their ire, do the glass panes rattle
bitter heartaches and soot-smeared hymns;
a cacophony of heresy screams from the center
where pastoral eyes and timidly wounded children
were demanded to watch the burning of their ilk
like dirty laundry aired over a bonfire.

a jewel of culture, where trade is all faith and no fathom
they cannot allow nor tolerate those that chose
to follow a love they will not understand.

―――― Ω ――――

the steady hand of dionysos

have you ever tasted the wine
from sun-kissed grapes that run through our vines?
lo, the revelry that flourishes under my hand—
we drink deep in thanks every twilight,
and come morn, we lie grateful in the dirt,
the smallest of fires burning inside us with pleasure;
the moon never taught me so much
about your body before,
I must give thanks for the stupor you have put me in.
your laurel crown of plenty has smoothed my features
a river of plying kisses and softened beds,

you would never guess olympus was ruled by immortals,
the way we savour mankind.

achelois

bring me your sick, your wounded and broken
bathe their bruises in my pools,
where the shattered and bleeding will rest
no harm brought to their aching bones.
my tenets reverberating within:
care for the sick. pray for the wild.
we are all children of the moon while here.

the ancestors will guide them,
gods will keep a watchful eye
as I return your pain to the earth,
wretched and weary with the thought of a burdened
eternity.

lay your scars at my altar and pray for forgiveness
I shall carry the call of mercy betwixt my shoulders
lest I fail in my duty to honor the injured.

bare branches

the earth beats within my bones
a warrior's call to deep roots;
I was something more, in another life
sparking and spitting with magick, ancient and pointed—
one that wrote ballads for courts, slunk through perfumed shadows,
arm-wrestled titans and out-witted mages.
the heart that resides in my chest
harbours dreams, desires, life;
you cannot fathom the well I may touch
nor the strength I will lend,
the triumph I will gift.
but travel, we will.
dark-lit roads await our sunny visages.

_____ Ω _____
evermore over eternity

every echo is an epiphany of the essence you ended with me;
she calls for evermore,
deep within the guilt-ridden reminder
of their every step towards her,
and it is with great trepidation
that the last of their kind lay down the guns
that have extinguished so many of her kind.

_____ Ω _____

we led the world, once

it's a depraved tango that we waltz across the wastelands
edging towards desperation and star-spangled wounds,
twilight eyes turned down to pits of labour and the forsaken.

_____ Ω _____
twenty-twenty-two

threaded silence hangs in the air
humid, hoping for the right angle;
a single shot pierces the veil
and now we are known.

_____ Ω _____
smashing atoms

tilted tarot, an axis hanging by a thread
while countless eyes grasp silently at a neon sky
praying for a saviour—
think could you ever be a saviour?

hidden in plain view, she wraps the cables of greatness
around fists ready for war, a divided mind
but singular in purpose.

three choices await her — *them*
while a burning horizon spreads rapidly outward.
only two more steps into the light,
and one heart to fill, severed down the center.

———— Ω ————
be angry, for that is what moves

be desperate for your home—
how can you watch, resting on your laurels?
only giving what makes others feel better
about themselves

this is a war on war;
while the ground is buried and people
are on fire,
swathes of humanity all want to act
but when will it be time
to take action instead
of giving thoughts and prayers?

a hole in the sky
in the ground
through the trees,
a catalyst of what is yet to come
and the few that want to mend it
always feel like it is still far too few.

woe unto the creature
that became greedy and gave us coin
woe unto the creature
that stood still while the world collapsed
woe unto us
for we sit and watch while
the uneducated elders deem us
lazy, unworthy, not as enlightened as the past

the past is broken,
mired in the hate of skin colour
and lineage
and who held the most coin,
when coin is the least of nature's issues
with us all.

when the guardians that swore to protect us,
the peacekeepers and governance
fail, turn a blind eye, are too scared to act,
who will rise and set them straight?
and who will say no, it is time to save all?

while the sum of us cry foul,
the newsfeed tells us where we are losing—
could someone share if we're succeeding too?
or are those words too many,
and without enough voices?

an eye for an eye once worked,
for a time,
when the snow was universal and
the hostility was for the apex

we broke walls with hearts years before
and yet we want to raise more;
watch as it murders itself,
one mass shooting
one human right
one treason
one war
at a time.

annual serenity

the yearly rolling of the scroll has fallen upon us
the earthy scent of incense hovers like
the warm glow of lantern light, washes our faces;
whispers of wind rinse the graves of their leaves
and we wait in anticipation
to be born anew in that big, black, empty sea.
we have kept ourselves free, even in the darkest of nights
for you were always my little light;

and so my wayward star,
you who have carried me so far —
will you come with me now
into the great beyond,
where dreams and nightmares lie in wait,
ready to pounce should you choose their fate?

Ω
an older soul, i.

the touch of marble never left
the soles of my feet;
I could hear the raucous laughter in the courtyard
where Dionysos prevailed tonight
like any night
I was but a victory, an exotic jewel
a spoil of war, admired and shunned
little more than a piece of flesh
to be clung to; a fertile field
for seed to be sown.
I hated it.
but no more.
the night of the celebration—
another bloody battle won, no doubt
it gifted me the second I needed
to end the golden cage that held me prisoner,
Athena help me.
like dear Julius at the Senate
my sweet husband fell to the sting of a dagger
consumed by wine and intoxicated by prostitutes
there is no love for me,
only patriarchal lust for his cursed lineage
well, husband of mine, your lust will be slaked
for you will meet your heavenly family by my hand
and settle the poison that has leaked into my heart
since you kidnapped me
used me
picked me clean.
the tables of fortune are not in your favour
and I will be free, free to run and start anew.
and should your brother-in-arms come for me
be sure to tell them the priestess of Athens
will not spare them from her wrath for centuries to come.

_____ Ω _____
rewriting sanity

chained daisies, leaning over the railing
patio of silverwood, pillars of ash
the finest weave of silk and cotton

dashed against the cobbles,
left for the rain under the Sistine
the chants of the sacred ring and die
on the ears of the holy,

no sacred union of light
a wash of mists and turn of phrase,
left me unconscious,
dead before pronounced;
how many years did it take
to tell the children,

"this is how you release the beast inside"?

―――― Ω ――――
an older soul, ii.

the sands of time are fraught with secrets and defiled love. the queen of the Nile has sat upon Egypt's throne for far longer than any man of letters has felt lust for a woman he can only watch from afar, in crowds of prostrated citizens; each of their bodies bent on my blessing She Who Lets the Nile Run.
but one cheated those far worthier of my love and praise, and stole into my heart one moonlit night; his pretense so innocent, but before midnight we had fallen to my bed in a heated dance, while the torches flicker into the sunrise. it was many sunrises of endless nights
before the poison was laid, the wily cobra that he was.
the men of my time were pale, but pets to a woman of
the gods; and yet the disgraced had nothing to lose and were favored by the heel of Anubis; succeed or die trying. his sickly-sweet verbiage, lies of the lunatics and jealous, were spilt onto my pillow each night, brimming with the confidence that only a court jester could muster in such a situation.
such heat radiated from this
selfish shell of subject
death awaited me
Anubis was so
impatient.
but not
the Nile.
the sands of time

hold fast to the queen
like the children I had borne
and like the cobra I coveted, my
fangs were long ready for his destruction;
each lie another chain on his wrists, and every
fountain of dishonour another glyph on the tomb
that
awaited his broken form. the fate that he had
deceived to
avoid now waited with honeyed words and curved
dagger; strength left his body like the koi dodging the net in the
pond, but
all fish must be caught someday, or die alone in the murk;
the citizens of the golden city had always known their
queen was not of this world — denizen of the
heavens,
when the body of the cold-blooded cobra was
found
it was set in unwritten stone that none could
disguise deceit with delight, nor love with
lies. and as the funeral procession made
its way through the winding streets of
the seaside paradise, none forgot
the power that had struck him
to the dust; none had nor
will forget the love
that flowed through the queen of the Nile,
for my people and their freedom. the night
would
scream for the soul of the defiler, left to be judged
by the scales of Osiris, all too aware that Amenti
would be feasting on the heart of the dead, lost to the Fields of
Reeds

_____ Ω _____

an older soul, iii.

the wind yowled like an angry housecat
and snow whipped my face,
cold hard shards of ice slicing my skin
but I stood, still;
the furs of Fenrir's children shielding my shoulders
whilst the shield of Járnviðr cradled my forearm,
the distance war cries of the enemies resonated off the cliffs of
Skaði
spooking the horses at the anticipation
of an av a l a n c h   e
but my warriors were sharp as new flint—
Odin's blessing burned in their hearts,
and Freyja's swallowed mine
we sat on a peak of Skaði's home, praying to the jotunn
for peace but for the moment.

the warriors of our seaside city were loyal—
they could hold fast to their honour
longer than a mother could hold her son back from horses.
I was proud to lead them, wielding my sword as swiftly
as Sigurðr wielded Hrotti in the days of old.

the jotunn goddess heard our prayers that moonrise
as Freyja led our sword-arms to bathe
in the blood of the enemies;
we took no prisoners that night,
and feasted heartily upon returning to our home
drinking to the powers that be for our glorious battle;
the enemy would not be so foolish to try a raid
while the Ulfheðnar still held a sword.

demonology

remember remember
the whispers of november —

but wait, this isn't a revolution
it's not even a rebellion
your white flag doesn't drop anything but morale
the one-man army of nothing

staggered steps and dried tongues,
cracked lips begging for Legion
for we are many
and the Unnamed is just many of our names

heavy heart and lightened shoulders
apostle of darkness and savior only of children
step into the parlour
your guardian angel alive

a train ticket to home,
small steps childishly dancing
are you real?
if you are, then I am

and the screaming finally ceases

to conquer one's demons,
you must first accept that heaven and hell
are not constructs of the world
but of mankind.

Ω
wands up

your face had many names,
each one a ring in the tree of your life;
a paragon in the arts, a kind voice in the wind   you
were the lighthouse in the fog,
the booming presence from above,
the firework display in Germany,
and the wizard who struck Muggle gold
in the hearts of millions;
the laughter in your halls will cease
to be moved to a higher place,
the kindness you gave to all
will be expedited to the world

I will remember you throughout the ages,
bringing my childhood to life on the silver screen
with your cloak darker than night,
but a plot as thick and bright
as the summer sun in Alaska.
you gifted secrets through your acting,
displaying the greatest form of history you could;
that even those deemed *moste wicked* and *traitorous*,
are not all they seem;

for help can always be given to those
who need it at Hogwarts,
and happiness may always be found in the darkest of times,
when one only remembers to turn on the light;
there will be a bounty of wishes to bring you back
because everyone dies too young
and all the magic in the world
cannot express how much we will love and miss you
always.

written in memory of Alan Rickman. my wand is up for you,
Housemaster

I am the elements

you have all held the smooth iron
of weathered bark, solid and light
you have felt the old strength that radiates
like komorebi through your fingertips;
you have tasted the air around the riverbank
clear and cold, fresh from its mountain escapades
it has the essence of new life and energy,
tangible to even the smallest of humans.
all have paid tribute to the brimstone
of the lightning storm, Zeus' horses
dancing through the hemisphere;
all have witnessed the terrible beauty
of the hurricane, she who stops for no man—

I am the elements, strong and nurturing,
relentless and immovable, proud and free.
the winter winds caress me,
the summer breeze carries me,
the spring hails my presence,
and the autumn is my crown —
I am the elements, and I am whole.

──── Ω ────
syzygy

the feeling of inexplicable serendipity; ineffable
the embodiment of being explicitly ethereal is uncontainable
the wisps and fireflies who cavort among them
while the petrichor enveloped the dozen or so of her senses —
they will never find her again,
lost and found among the ruins of another lifetime
flitting like a fox from den to hole to hell;
she grew up iridescently in a land filled
with evocative illicit exploits and external heartbeats.
always in the in-between of solitude and oblivion,
wholeheartedly sharing, unwittingly caring
spending most days supine, suspended between her old memories
and the ones yet to come, if she traveled that far.

and now here she stood, a radiant cynosure
she had crawled at the feet of men and mice,
drowned in a polluted deluge of human spirit,
set ablaze a crestfallen planet, home of the demure and dejected,
to bring back life to her race, the motley bunch they had been,
given them a new lease on life, given them a fervor for the unknown again;
they stood on the cusp of fairy tales and legends,
and she knew, in the wells of her heart
that she had been born to live among the stars
in this life and the next.

moiety

we will collide, all of us,
in the mason jar of the universe,
surrounded by the efflorescent stars
and the ephemeral call of the soul
the very marrow of your bones telling you stories
of when you were a child, long ago, in a faraway place
you would run the fields, fly with the kites;
to now, in a fugacious moment, you are here
beholding the stars with them in your eyes,
but you exist and you are here to witness the birth
and death of the heart and mind and soul over and over
until the very end; the very fabric of the universe
has come undone, a downy throw on your shoulders
opulent and extravagant; you wear Orion so beautifully,
did you know?
so don't ever forget that even when the night is bleak,
your mind is lithe and willing to forget that you are the world
in a form that is all your own;
do not forget that you, in all your glory, old and young,
you are sempiternal — you are the stars best eyes, strongest heart
swiftest kiss; you are the stars, and they will bow to you.

we're all created from stardust

do you remember
the night you stared at the stars
and felt more?
do you remember the feeling
that coursed through your blood and bones,
and you felt the shimmer inside you?
you can feel it now,
lit like a candle that burns slow
the choir that starts softly inside
you understand when I tell you
that the Northern Lights
awakens in your eyes
whenever you smile into the mirror,
and the Milky Way ignites the darkness
that will never reach you

we are made of stardust,
you and I
bold, with the courage of stars;
unique and exquisite is our existence
as if the universe intended for its beauty
to be seen by only our eyes.

the soul: a past life portal

the breadth of knowledge
spans countless eons
and the bamboo lanes that I walk
are all too familiar to me;
except not.
I find places that feel like home,
only to find I had never been there before.
I experience exquisite moments,
only to find that it had never happened before.
I meet people that feel like long lost family and friends,
only to find that we have never spoken before that moment.

so, I explore further
delving into my soul
to find the doors that have long closed
and peer through their key holes;
to find myself?
perhaps
to find myself again?
well, that's the journey, isn't it?

the pen and the sword

betwixt the eye of the storm and the shorelines of paradise
the sand of a thousand dreams gently casts its net
its caster fixed with a golden crown of hopes
and none of these are unreachable,
and none of these are lies,

what was once a wall is now a lean-to
it is not difficult to overcome,
but rather making the decision to do so
thrice the lines have made themselves known
don't leave them calling back

your queen may praise the laws of the land
whilst your enemies are blind in the dark
but heaven forbid you forget where your allies lie
where your heart resides
where your hearth can be found

the world may make itself
but it does not make the man
and those rules are set only by pen
and sometimes by slender blade,
but always by the wielder.

originally penned in 2017, a birthday gift for my dear friend, Ian.

_____ Ω _____
a fight to the man

angelic faces under cuts and abrasions
dipping low to scour the seas,
naval strength that forges the waves
into anvils of cold calculations

taken away from the teat of sanity
engorged on fantasies left to fester
from whence we came
struggles the barbs of hatred

the cynosure is waiting,
man's time spins on less than a dime
does so little matter
that our raconteurs have abandoned us?

bring forward the speech
that will wash our hearts with sense
in the wistfulness
that only history can remind us of.

we will not stumble

greyed out opinions for greyed out facts,
a letter in the mail lost in the approaching storm;
at the edge of the globe
the end looks far too close.

shaking hands on bloody pen, mightier than thou
a halo of smoke sits around shoulders
that have carried mock saviors,
vintage lies, and modern excuses
in a grasping attempt for something mellifluous

we are not statues of marble
nor babes of an ancient,
in the recesses of our chests
is hiraeth,
waiting for its epoch to be written

nothing is out of reach,
we are at the carfax
one and all
there is no epiphany
do not let our denouement
be one of a stranger's wanderlust.

history won't forget you

the echoes of ancient warbling
jilting priests of faith
abandoning the path for the pleasure

what would the matriarch say as she lay in eternal sleep
cloistered and deafened by the archaic rumblings of incest
ensconced in a man-made prison of her own work?

he who lingered on the precipice of denial
his peripheral skewered with what-ifs
he took the bludgeoning blame boldly

fatally

a crushing sweep of dry tinder lit like the banquet halls
surrender had been sweet, until defeat
serpents tasting the salty air in the baths of blood

as roman ships crush the gods beneath their heels
sinking, unknowingly, into history and its winner's cornucopia
blinded by gold, unseeing of the knife in the dark

drowning in droplets

we've never needed a rope
already anchored to the bottom, drop down
engine died, crept into the salt air

we didn't know better, left the map behind
lost like we were on mount everest
caved in and concave

we didn't know the tide was going to rise
never watched the weather report before
why, when monsoon season felt like every day

terrible scars in the skies reflected in our eyes
adrift on the worst river
close to shore, we don't care enough yet

held back again by the weight of the anchor
sitting in the middle of the boat now
and neither of us will toss it out

_____ Ω _____
determined footsteps on slick obsidian

She wishes you had stayed in the guestroom. Her feet are treading the floor heavily, black as coal, glassy where you lay. She can't be by your side, can't let herself flow from her to you any longer. It burns the night and slaughters the dawn, and she is just so lost, so lost within you. There are fingertips that make her lose her religions, but you couldn't leave her alone. You couldn't leave her alone because you said you loved her and she said it too, but what does that mean when you can't be in the same room?

The guestroom, the guestroom, all her fault — she got naked first. You were right next door, and she could feel you through the walls. All her fault. The obsidian calls to her, but so do you. Underneath your teeth, it reminded her of home, breaking her apart like a jeweler looking for flaws in a diamond, like false gods answering your prayers.

She keeps thinking about you in the worst ways, just laid out, your footsteps running down her arms. You never told her what you thought about obsidian, did you? Did you know it lends strength, wards of pressures, excess stress — the excess of what oozed from the guestroom. She wished you had left her tongue alone, left her alone naked in the rug of fire, wrapped around the consciousness of a god with entrails leaking from the eyes. Sifting through her soul like a dog in a garbage bin. Coyotes don't know what excess means, but they see a dying breed when they come upon it. You are the dying breed, and it's all her fault. The obsidian floor did nothing to save you, it left you alone. What kind of witch is abandoned by her own? It's all your fault, and she stayed in the guestroom. You pinned her down, teeth in her hair, ripping her heart into diamond shards and carried her to bed.

She let the night stay black, turned you away and didn't look back. You brought obsidian to her door, just leave it on the floor. Her arms are cold, heart is black, feet are weary. She lost herself, and she doesn't want her back, I think. No, she doesn't want her back.

She's behind me, isn't she?

_____ Ω _____
[hiberna]v.[incuba]tion

seeping into the niche she has hollowed
wary of familiar faces,
she treads the coal-laden path
ironbark in one hand, fate in the other
casting aside the notion of pride
and replacing it with drive;
there is no waiting for the sleepers

―――― Ω ――――
far too late

desperation breeds
consolation, services
inspiration, requires
justification.

inspiration

all this movement,
still not on time
trying to record my thoughts
and they just don't rhyme.

entitled venom

and if I must think of you
I do so unwillingly, with barbs in my teeth
possessive of another ghost,
there is no purchase for you here, demon
what you wrongfully threw into the river
dragged itself back to me
and let me soak up the wounds while singing hymns
praise the goddess that she no longer battered

so, if I must think of you,
I will do so unwillingly
and with stakes in my hands.

smashed tea

sometimes, we are not the correct fit
for another human being
and sometimes, we are beleaguered.

there are people in the world that are too angry
too hurt
too scared

and sometimes you need the propinquity to want to move on
and it was this that I forgot
and it was because of this that I was burned

it does not mean you are broken,
it does not mean either are
it simply means
we must move on

and I wish there wasn't blame.
and I had hoped there would be mercy.
left afloat and unarmed
the captain calling, 'let go!'
and I didn't know how—

but sometimes we are not the right person
and sometimes it's just a bad fit.
but sometimes we can help people
and that makes it all worth it.

izanagi's cavern

when you murmur the name of the holy—
whomsoever you douse in that light—
do you feel the air still
or the waters calm?

grace and existential peonies gather at your feet
as the perpetual loop of stars shutting their eyes
and reawakening on the other side of the cosmos
attending to the needs of the royal and lush

you are favoured, star kin, and the moon dances on your brow
each pillowed step another in the right direction
each cherished petal a gold thread in your tapestry
zither in the hall, harp in the observatory

and you call down the heavens when tears fall
wishing you were in the embrace of your ancestors
hoping your mortality has brought them honor
praying your birthright has been given its justice.

_____ Ω _____
inevitably

and just when did you think I disappeared?
the radio was tuned low, not off
the sounds were gentle, listen softly
the waves of innovation rise in the pool of humanity
and I have touched the tip barely;

but blessed be that journey I took
for I learned many a thing in that moon cycle
and I look to the horizon as I mold it to my liking

the crisp scent of change is on the wind,
and it excites me to see what it will hold—
just what will it become?

but let us revel together,
for that is what friendship is;
I was not lost, and nor did I need to be found
the in-between is where I lived
sometimes up, sometimes down.

―――― Ω ――――
ad infinitum

they teased out the idea that sanity
comes with a price,
affordable and reasonable—
the fine print reminded her
that even in the direst of straits,
there is always a monger to be found;

enriched in the insanity of reality
where people are still human, left behind
in the realm of possibility and change
there are fingers grasping for
just one chance, one more turn
never to be seen, always the carrot and stick

type As stepping over type Bs
a morose air in the way they lift their leg
and watch as the rest fall away,
destined for dealings unknown
and contracts never fulfilled.

as a child, you knew you would rise

the throne of the lost has been vacated
and in its place sits a sword of stone
the story of royalty should it be lifted
is now a warning for pretenders;

ye who take the burden
who seeks redemption in darkness
don't carry forward
lest your own heart grow stony
and lost upon your brow, will the crown sit

the lost are now found,
relinquished for purpose
and the time has come to rise above the shadows
the spirit of man never dying

pray heed the mourning calls of time
and look towards the horizon instead
there is no warrior who will sink their teeth into black
when there is the light to feast upon

six ways split into sevens

betrothed to the frozen rain and in love with the empty skies;
six hours 'til dusk, you never caught your sleep
and each inch taken was another mile lost
tiptoed around the tulips, loathe to disturb peace
even as the clouds held back their thunder for you

five stars 'til twilight, and you stood behind me
a fight to the empty abyss
but we always stood together,
a cornucopia of risen memories
bubbling to the surface

four kisses 'til dawn, holding out like a shark at the table
oh, the trouble that held back your hair,
did you even get her name?
twisted turns and straight narrows
the map to you was never an easy road to follow

three ways 'til the morning, and it was always worth it
tenfold when you had coffee on the wooden stairs ready
tornado warnings gave you that old gleam again
your heart was longing for war,
the peace you fought for was never enough

two ways 'til the light, and you held your gun once more
shining like the Round Table, but filled to the brim with sin
the preacher hoarse will recompense for you
even as you cut down the masses that pray to no one

one way 'til the darkness, and you stood before me
our candle flickering like your heart
burning like my eyes, filled with coarse smoke;
what labyrinth had we created
a picture—perfect conclusion to the turmoil and saintly
never long for this world, always grasping at eternity

zero dawn for the holy, breaking ground for hell,
tear the rift at its seams and unleash your hounds
hear the roar of the earth and then,
perhaps,
it will be enough.

Ω
the homeless deity

the origins of the peasant
are lost when they become something more;
but does that old woman appear to be
a homeless deity?

in the unrest of the civil,
shaking closets do not always mean hidden children
though the beginnings are sometimes begat there –
the skeletons that hide from the politics
will walk the earth
fueled by the overripe hatred of the people
but if the stars do align and the angels still do not sing
will your faith waiver or simply stall?
for why should the preacher be a liar
when he was only speaking another's truth?
truth is circumstantial to your reality
we take it all at face value,
even if the face is made of gold

a partition of innocence and new ideas
breeds a new generation of so-called blasphemers
by the people who once carried lizard tails as spiritual wards
so we stand and watch the world burn, while a new one
is born under our feet.
there is magic in my veins, thick with the notion
that there is always something wonderful to be peered upon
a grime-stricken window does not mean light exists nowhere
but the lamp
while a moth does not always entail death in the hands of fire

so, freedom-fighter, sunlight on the witch's helm and smoke in
your mouth
that door isn't going to kick itself in,
that philosophy isn't going to debate itself
are you going to humanize us all

or will you join the mutiny on board?

into the woods

and I am etched in gold,
and that is all I have ever been told

let me grow old
I want my story to unfold.

avatar of gaea

gather round, listen
I will tell you a secret;

would you think the mountains were still
if the clouds hugged them so tight,
can you hear its heartbeat?
that distant echo in the valley,
the still breathing of the gods

there is life in all things
do not discount the small instances
what better way to eliminate the fog
than wiping away the tears of the earth?

a wintry thursday morning

and the sidewalks are chipped with frost and footprints,
the towers shimmer gold in the rising sun
the rivers are frozen, but not quite solid;
and the wintery air hurts my cheeks,
the train runs by with cargo for the countryside
and there are mittens and toques in a thin sea of commuters.
there are cars below, a truck driver with his load for the day
a mother running for the door with her stroller, though she passed two on the way
and there's dirty snow water sliding down the floor while the masses leave
salt crystals left on the platforms because no one wants to lose it today.
and the greenhouse is hiring, seedlets arrayed in their backyard
the tree branches are hanging icicles out to dry
and the brush below is a wonderland of wading if only we had more time;
the turn of a newspaper, the shuffle of wet boots
the hustle and bustle of downtown.
and it's all for something, but we're just not sure what yet
the destination is determined, but are we really going there now or right now?

and all I want to do is
sit on a snowy rooftop with a coffee
and observe the world going by.

Ω
assassin's artistry

feel the shadowing abyss
we play the imitation game so well
dance the dance, you taught me and I never fell
a survivor is born every day, but the night is always young
and we play the imitation game so well,
each step so careful, a delicate foot on each rung

two hundred years of moving forward,
but we cannot stop now
no, don't just try to avert — just plow!
one two three, one two three
we turn like a ballerina,
ah, the days of basic training
thrown into the icy waters of the marina

tiptoe now, the little spider can see you
we play the imitation game too well
and I have forgotten whose side you are on
until the black curtain falls behind us
and I am the one with the knife in your back

keep going, keep moving
your waltz is nowhere near mine
my dear partner lost to crime
I'll surrender your body with mine
if only they catch me crossing the line.

teething

set in stone,
rushed to the bone,
when can we go home?

dry cobblestone to soaking wood

stormy waters rush from the sea
blood on the cobblestones
we bathe in it, the wretched and wicked
an eye for a coin, cheapest bargain made today
and yet the gold couldn't save her sight

twisted knife in a rib cage
we are bound by cold lashings and thunderous oaths

walk the deck, caress the steel
elbows deep in hell

oh, but it only gets better from here.

knit one, pearl too

there is a science to knitting,
much like bone
and if you are a beginner, we can learn together
I was a weaver in a past life
a seer in a past life

and we wove stars together,
broke hearts together,
started wars together

and when Rome came crashing down
I saved the ashes to build anew with you
and when the Nile came rushing inwards
we sailed the banks and navigated the torrents

the astronomical repercussions of us meeting
are ones I care not to indulge myself in
we are the cluster stitchers, not fate
I follow no path but the one I blaze

and in the case of two times ten,
I would say you are a million and one
and the echo of my mistakes
will, with hope, keep you from coming undone

when we reach the emerald hills
far into the west
I hope the second sun touches your cheeks
and you are reminded of the flare that began it all

the pariah's wound

catastrophic conduit, assemblage in lilac
never had I brooded so fiercely over nothing
elixirs I have not drank wishing for more, more

don't you d a r e scream for my heart
when you disrespect my lungs
each and every laugh imbued with the love and hatred
of too many generations left alive
[and too many left for dead]

the least I could do was let the sun revive your bones
the most I could do was let your teeth crumble
the consequences of my almost actions ring in my hands
and I have to pull back to keep it from falling apart

the good in me is the good in you,
but the hell in me resonates in you
chipped china in a charity shop
leave it all on the shelf when the storm comes
all I want to hear is my world shattering.

Ω

an untitled life

Q: Dear Abby, is it proper for women to be learned?

remember in the old days, when women had no voice?
their chords shut tight, the hand of the man choking her
what ever happened to good, old-fashioned duels
the ones in books that were forbidden;
chivalry was never dead, he always held the door to her coffin open first
"after you, milady"—

can't say I remember the old days,
but there was once someone who gave away rights like candy
and they didn't even believe in halloween;
I would say in between the slaughtering of good people
and the emancipation of a country,
that a woman who can read is bound to profit a soul, not her own
before being turned down for the night, the endless night,
so don't forget to leave the lamp on
while I study this chart on female anatomy,
can't have anyone knowing you can think for yourself, you know?

dear concept

dear concept,

you marvelous little idea, you thrive in so many ways
entering the portals of hands and arriving in the landscapes of minds
whatever did you do with the drapes, they're mismatched and tattered?
didn't we say if you needed a hand, just let us know?

but that's not why I wrote; it is long overdue, but I just needed to say
thank you
for teaching the right ways of conduct, of course!
never have I driven to a conclusion so quickly without backup,
never have I pointed a finger without knowledge so fast,
but where would I be without the intellectual conversation of anger?

it was too much for you to deliver the promise of a life,
and handed over a barely concealed lie,
but such are promises and life, no?
the tenants before I, loved this house much more than I had ever could
but here I am, hoping I will do it justice.

please don't write, I will write you.
I owe you money, but I'm unsure why – you said it was square,
but your sister said it was triple? please clarify.
yours,
thoughts

burning firs

trouble maker,
you walk the finest line
whispers in the dark, coming to light
and the tallest tree is always the first to fall

but a forest survives the winter,
while the loner exudes arrogance and withers
frustrated in the ways of the world
but there is no lie when we say
fire burns needles
and you are in a matchstick bed.

instinction

we traded our sharp hands for a sharp mind
but what did we lose in the process?

a reflex—
a higher purpose?

what about a common goal?

the wonders of mankind stretch from evolution
to religious devotion

but what of our physical?
did we trade our ability to keep up
for our ability to race?

―――― Ω ――――
m (aiden) [ast]

the devil's in the details,
etched into my DNA
every secret spilled; every subtle nod noticed
and the sound of the bells at the docks
ring in my ears, like a lover's whisper
I cared not for the executioner and his mistress
she's as sharp as a whip, sometimes sharper
I can't be bothered to ask after her
not after what they did to my Arn—

and so, the bells keep me content
my compass keeps me calm
my sails carry me wherever I wish

and my pirate's love song is never over,
so long as the salt spray crashes over me
so long as the deck creaks in the moonlight
so long as there's a bounty upon me.

Ω
blindside the seer

soothsayers should not see themselves,
leave the path untouched
lest you corrupt your own sight;

seen too many battles
and almost as many victories,
trying to keep the roof patched
as arrows of fire sink into straw

soothsayers should be blind,
let fate draw the lines behind closed lids—
believe.

I want to believe.

do not fall in love with a writer

Do not fall in love with a writer.

They can paint with colors that you have never heard of before, and create new worlds with one strong emotion. They have a heart that outstrips any fuel source, and is full of butterflies and frustration. They come alive in the early hours of morning, when the only noise they can perceive is the one coming from your sleeping form; they sleep when the sunlight isn't quite in the shape they need to work their magic. They can conjure up the simplest of cliches, and leave you in a burning wake of words, singeing your arms and eyes with embers of passion and misnomers. They have moments of weakness, and brief seconds of strength, and the only thing they will keep to themselves is how many times they said, "You can do better than that". They've fallen in love with the impossible, and wept over the improbable. Their wishes comprise of fanatical love tales, and the harmonizing of fates that were almost lost to the dusty shelves of old book stores. Ink once flowed through their veins, replaced now with the telltale signs of the clinically insane; one with the world of imagination.

Do not fall in love with these writers, for they will smother you in complicated words and rumpled paper, unbridled attention and time laid at your feet, willingly or not. They will kiss you a thousand times to make sure they record the correct flavor of you, write pages on the way you breathe when your eyes are closed. They understand cliches like the sun setting on your cheeks and starlight in your eyes, and can immortalize wounds like pieces of Da Vinci's art. Unbeknownst to you, your very fingertips will unlock places inside them that they have been waiting to dust for years, and they will use your soul until it becomes a dried leaf in the autumn wind. Snow storms and catastrophic earthquakes mold their faces, lined with the visions of heartstrings and dark alleys. They will envision waterfall kisses, and embraces pooled in moonlight — cliffhanging their demons beside your own and wondering if they will help or hinder themselves. Lightning storms gather around their throats when they speak your name, and the atmosphere is charged with the static of what should come from them next.

If you should fall in love with them, understand you will have a legacy that will last a lifetime. The halls of their mind will reverberate with your name, and a single touch will venture into volcanic territory, where they have hidden you away in their ever—green glade. They will build monuments in your name, and shout them into the cavernous masses that envelope their creations. Every deduction, every thought, every question they ever had about you will become a matter of who and how it will be alive to them in just the right way. You become their perfect universe, a paradox of the one their physical lives play out. They will love every piece of you, from the way you say hello to strangers, to how you brush your teeth at night. They will find every piece of you fascinating, from how you put your socks on to the way you push your glasses further up your nose. Things like tying your shoes, drinking coffee, running an errand — all fodder for an extraordinary article of continuous love and intrigue. Their tired eyes will drink you in like the fountain of youth, and their smile will be rare, but will always play when yours does. They will capture the moments you call 'every day', and configure them into artwork. They will love your storms, your rainfall, your sunshine and green valleys, and even your blizzards and tornadoes. And they will never stop writing about you.

miss mittens & her kittens

miss mittens and her two kittens
lived in the rainy back lane
they loved fishy heads, fluffy socks for their bed
and their fur brushed out like a mane

the old man on the porch was allergic to cats,
and walked the lane every day
he'd aim a swift kick, they'd jump back a tick
and curse them on his walk to the bay

one day the old man's kick aimed true
and miss mittens' kitten had a bruised back
the old man snickered while the cats scarpered quicker,
his hands tucked into his brown slacks

a week went by and the old man was pleased
he saw no sign of cat, no fish heads or socks
no furry manes, mice, or cat games
for he had the eyes of a hawk

but as he walked the shore of the bay,
he tripped and fell into the water
he couldn't swim – no one could save him but him!
and out of the corner of his eye, he spotted a small squatter

the water, it ate him right up
his brown slacks in tow, his life now unwritten
and on the shore, with furry manes and cat games
was miss mittens and her two kittens

──── Ω ────
water-logged chest

and each time my chest tightens just a bit more,
thoughts a Gordian knot of horrors
turn it off, please, just turn it off—

reprieve is a paradise, and lost words a treasure
and yet, when I speak, I go only to Hell first.

bloody, I'm bloody
bandages wrapped in barbs and hurt
offering a salve that will eventually
numb me

numb is not alive, though,
and I just want to be alive.

a musing

what is woven into the web of life
depends greatly on the materials you use.

the nonexistent shed

hand me that wrench,
pass me that nail
it's quarter past eleven when I see
it's to no avail

a push and a pull,
two step, left and right
lean on me once,
but choked me twice

the bible in the desk
but a sin in your eyes
what's the difference between me and you?
ah yes, a selfish lie.

open bar

double shot of vodka,
my watch is blinking 1700 hours—
stood me up again,
and I have come to expect nothing but the best
from your behaviour.

the dust in the sills,
the age in the bartender's smile
the scum that is sitting behind me
the exit sign that flickers slowly

it's all a part of my design,
when should I make the change?
when I'm toppled over a trash can
wondering if I should drink more water while my insides empty?

I need a whole lot of convincing
and a whole lot of cash
and when you find me sitting down at the slots
razing my chips to the ground
maybe you'll remember that at 1701 hours,
you left me behind again.

oh

sat beside her on the bus
freshly inked arm, she kept glancing it over
as if it would sneak away
I could smell her light perfume—
it felt like it suited her inside and out;
she had a casual demeanor that made my heart say,
oh
and for two moments I was in fascinating lust.
we would stroll English Bay, her skateboard and my bike
(I'd learn to ride, of course)
she would play music while I wrote to her heavy rock
convincing me to get another piercing
"it doesn't hurt, y'know", a smirk on her face

and then I got off the bus,
remembered where I was,
took a deep breath,
and said "*oh*."

―――― Ω ――――
a long way down

she asked me to, while you were asleep
waited with tearful eyes until I awoke to her calls
and I cannot deny my faithful
when they come so willingly
you had never made her scream before;

she wanted me to, while you were away
offered herself upon my altar
she was paltry and universal
tendrils of hair lay in my lap,
oh, how she wandered my fields with awe

I would keep that wonder for myself

she needed me to, to discard the emptiness you had left
tucked away in the cage you had thrown away the key to
my dear, I would gladly grant your wish,
while she clamors into my lap,
I sink you to the beds below;
do say hello to my nephew when you reach hell.

_____ Ω _____
te[ch]apel

"the finest connections across the continent!"
or so I was told;

but the thousands of "more" pour into my screen
clogging my weather and changing my needs
made me wonder if it was necessary to have a plan
that streamlined the wants of the petty
and the pleading of the masses

and just once in a while, the phallic pose of bygones
threads through my eyes
and I must remind myself that no,
olympus is far, far behind

what was in it for me to be gun shy of a camera?
a little lip service drove me into the pockets of the wealthy
and the minds of the priests
you don't need a sabbatical when you have me.

Ω
a woman's heart

bathhouse number two, she reclined in her own tears
a rose petal or nine left on my shrine,
as she prayed for another sign;

how could I tell her he was a cicada in the summer,
a seasonal affliction to her soul?
he stole her smiles for sweet rolls
harboured her kisses for trade at the brothels

priestess of my temple, do not weep at my feet
he was never worthy of the towers to your heart
but perhaps *she* is worthy of making your bed?

broken heart

and what if I am the tempest, scouring the foam for your eyes?
do not pray for the best to come
if you do not know what the best of us will bring
you prayed for an outcome, not a resolution

and just as you left me in the fire, I too fell in love with the stakes
the pyre was a comfort, once upon a shore
now it fills the skies with the clouded reassurances
of a prolonged death; my sisters never had a chance

they say hell hath no fury like a woman scorned;
so, what does hell say when she rules it?

Ω
aphrosiren

in her palm it rested,
portal to every love
her lips could discover.
she texted back,
"come over, I need you"
and grinned at
the heart replies.
in her palm it buzzed
gently; twenty other suitors
pried.

as she basked
in their adoration,
in her palm it glowed,
brighter, brighter,
blinding.
so bright it became
audible, loud and
awful. her grip
tightened, her nails
pressed through the screen,
into each of their minds;
she drank deep of lives
she never lived.

an overwhelming sense of
underwhelming love
in her modern pantheon of
misunderstood wooers
and she was their muse;
her golden laurel glimmered
with the discarded cores of men
and women alike.
they sustained her,

though tears ran down her face
to the insistent beat of
why, why

the soft tinkle of waiting faces
held between the limbo of
'unread' and 'read'
in her carefully constructed temple
of would-be heroes and damsels
trying to save her heart;
what would a sword know about
leaving people waiting—
is that too close a question
to one's heart, she wondered.

equinox

can you feel it, like I do?
the whispers of harvest
tangible emotion of change and warmth

and every year I reminisce
the red leaves that have accompanied
some of my best smiles

old flames in a whirlwind of new leaves
heady life, whirling in temporary motions
when I yearned for knowledge,
it presented itself
in the shape of tempered pages,
corridors of voices
it swelled, and was my hearth

decades could dance by
and I would waltz to its music, for my thrum
resides in the beauty that is change
heralded by curling smoke
snow tipped mountains,
crunching leaves—

welcome home, autumn

Ω
a better beginning

tiptoe through the fields
of egg white and overfeeding
of newspaper clippings and exit signs
slip through the weavings of those alien to your senses
and run terror through when the alien comes to life
blissful paradise does not exist anymore
and peace comes with the price
of the brave
but to gain a universe
there must first be
a better beginning.

the remaining cornerstone

breathing dirty water
the marrow in my bones is telling me
we've landed in a natural disaster
the response teams are lost
what do we do?

wait for the morning.

and when the sun peeks out
do we wait for the fog to clear
and head out?
or trip through the wreckage?

_____ Ω _____
whispers in the brush

could you hear the rushing
the whistling through the grass
have you lost the senses that have preserved you
generation over generation?

recall your warrior, spirit—
you feel the drums, but can you taste them?

in the shadow of each other the people live.
but we cannot thrive without
the beat of our hearts

one hand takes
another gives
but when do you use both?
when it becomes too much—
and then you grab the torch and sword

"writing one's own obituary because you're mourning a profound part of yourself."

where one used to travel, worn was the path
now walk down the trail, gray grass beneath my feet
I miss my sense of innocence,
lost in the years of late-night phone calls
midnight tears
coalescent agony, brought to my knees
and the only way out was to score myself
who else would provide the sword?

she rests in an ash tree,
burdened and confused no longer
but oh, how I miss her smile.

hail, mary

she said three in a row,
breathing as labored as the construction worker chasing her
he swore she was dead meat, but
she told him she'd keep your word,
"I didn't see anything!"
mother of god, where were you now?
why couldn't you teach your sons to behave
why must women pay the price
for the ways of man?
where was your spirit now,
as he screamed at her back
footsteps pounding the pavement—
"get back here, mary!"
but oh, on the contrary
she was getting out of there

a holy hoax, only alleyways and trash bins greeted her
waiting to witness another dispute
another call
another scream

she said more than three hail marys this time
the sixth one turned into a marigold
and she saw things from thirty thousand feet—
life was strange, but so was flying
and though she was a pure soul, you can imagine
the hell that reigned down afterward
was nothing short of a holy war
what else does one do when a man kills your mother?

my grimoire

my favourite time of year,
fleshed out in apricot leaves and ginger skies
both as healthy as the real things—
the year's wheel is just as invigorating
as the one before

I am oft looking through the notes
scrawled in the margins to myself
and it is curious to see
the realism come to life — or is it
cynicism?
unimpeachable?
the catalysts that my fingers have become
swept away the fireflies in the night

I live by the burning fires now
onyx around my neck,
the stars in my eyes
the sermons have changed from light and love
to strength and stability,
the more primal aspect of the heart
but the message is still the same;

there are smudges and stones
snarls and demons, witchery and shadows
but there is the sun and the moon
within what you would call the dark
it is not so much transcendence as it is
resurrection
or would that be evolution?

―――― Ω ――――
rudimentary bio

sometimes I am woolly turtleneck,
khaki slacks and leather shoes
black jacket loosely around my shoulders in the autumn morning
waiting for the day to begin while it passes by.

sometimes I am yoga pants and hooded sweaters
ballerina flats worn from usage
shoulder bag slung the wrong way
a fantasy world before me, and mulling through my veins.

sometimes I am violet gowned
silver toed and clutch in hand
a face on a face, a drink for the evening's delights
wishing I was home, missing my bear-heart.

but mostly, I am the sparrow on my wrist,
the compass on my shoulder, the milky way
always pointing north
ad astra per aspera

I am long hair and small freckles,
graying eyes and crooked smile
a hum in my throat, the ever-worrisome bitch face
I swear I'm not mad, don't mind the turned down—
I am the feeling of worry, the anxious stare at the road
the relaxed smile when leaves fall
the flop of the blankets on the bed when it's cold

and sometimes
I am a writer.

———— Ω ————
in the write moment

whispers of the ether trickle through the cracks in the parchment
one drip at a time fell upon your knuckles as you wrote
and the whole time, you could feel
your magick flow.

──── Ω ────
friendly fire

save a penny
earn a pence,
we harken back to
the way we were
behind dark shades
don't play with fire,
friends

alive

don't forget to call tonight
don't forget to lock up tight
she's waiting for her moment
the chimney curling in, smoking

the thing inside of you comes alive
she draws it like a bow
it's seeping under the door frame
watch your step—

you're in the woods
you're all alone
you ran too far
forgot which way was home

silence is no comfort
your voice is hoarse
it's too late to say sorry—

the wolves come out to see the end.

Ω
fatal cold shoulder

she caught him hiding in the dark
promised he'd stay in place; "we'll never be apart"
she once prayed he would be there
couldn't imagine the whispers, beware

he shunned the night, held grudges against stars
broke fire against her memoirs
lighting up the wildwoods;
her home turned to cinders
she'll break more than fingers—

doubt cracked her windshield
eternity stepped back, couldn't make an appeal
the clouds creeped behind him
don't hang on too tight, let it skim;

the occult loved her when the stars faded
she could sleep in its blanket, left alone and jaded
but what was a human to immortality?
she would never tell him of that fatality.

_____ Ω _____
twenty minutes of dawn

There was a stretch of land, filled with the harvest of Mother Nature's bountiful corn. They shook in the breeze like a child with a tambourine, and the sound whistled over the tops of the stalks like a hot air balloon. The sun was the most brilliant azure on a late afternoon, so beautiful it made even the hardened of veterans realize just how small they were in the wide, wide world.

A path ran straight through the field, leading in a pattern that no one ever quite understood. But if you walked for long enough, you would come to a clearing, almost in a perfect square. A small house stood there; white washed rancher, sun burnt just as anything else could and would be in these parched lands. The window frame was cracked, splintered just enough that if you ran your fingers across it, you would come back scathed. The door was wide open, also in that dim white color that seemed to make up the house. You couldn't see inside properly, but it gave off the feel of a very old home, that had seemingly fell out of the sky to land where it sat now. A dirt path ran around the house, and a small garden lay at its side, with enough desert fauna in it to make it appear to be something from nothing. A dusty and beaten 'Welcome' mat lay at the front of it all to complete the picture.

And to the side of this picturesque house sat an old Cadillac. The burnished red color blended into the dying light that permeated the very air. Its tires were the color of chalky coal, and looked like they hadn't moved since it was built. The windows were rolled down, as if the car needed to breathe in the prairie air to move once more. The windshield was wholesome, if dirty, and small animal prints covered the left—hand side of the glass; someone called this vehicle home on cold nights. The leather seats were cracked and worn, and matched the leather steering wheel. Small pieces of duct tape were wrapped around the handle in some places, making you feel like that time your bike broke down at your best friend's place, and all you could do to fix it was wrap it with the duct tape your friend offered you. And on this old piece of history sat three girls. Perhaps only a year or two between each other from youngest to oldest, but they sat there nonetheless. They wore similar gowns, as if ready for bedtime. The tallest (perhaps not the eldest) wore a gown of purple, the hem trailing the bottoms of her knees. It hung comfortably on her shoulders, and was just barely starting to hug her hips as she grew into herself, and she stood near the hood, leaning against it to watch the sun go down. The middle child's gown was the color of sea foam off the Caribbean, or so I hear. It threw itself around her calves like a contemporary dancer, and fit her just the opposite, rustling against the trunk of the car where she sat. The shortest girl had a gown of beautiful blue, the color of the prairie skies on a hot summer afternoon. It flowed past her ankles onto the roof of the car, where she had settled herself contentedly to watch the spectacle of a dark colored rainbow while the sun bowed off stage.

There was hardly a sound to be heard, except the crickets and the soft breeze grazing the stalks. The girls watched, unblinkingly, hardly daring to move lest they miss something that could change their home. It was a scene out of a fantasy, and old western. Time was frozen here; there was no changing that.

A shooting star crossed the navy blue that was finally descending onto the fields, and the shortest (perhaps not the youngest) gave a trill of laughter, the sound so pleasing to the ear. It would remind one of the early morning birds that woke you up ever so quietly, that you just knew it couldn't have been anything else. Their eyes were turned to the skies even more intently now, focused on spotting the falling star before it burned up in our atmosphere. To imagine such an otherworldly thing could disintegrate so gracefully in the view of our very plain eyes, was such a concept that wouldn't be dreamed of by those girls until very later in their lives.

The moon began its ascent into the sky, crawling from the horizon after it had kissed the sun goodnight. A crescent moon, divine and destined to leave Earth dwellers in awe for many, many moons to come. Its finely shaped contours easily outstripped any mortal beauty; who could match the curves of the sculpted Luna? She was finer than all the others in that visible sky. Many years from now, in a house similar to this one, the girls would discuss the moon and her properties, and their husbands would wonder just how they could talk about something so alien as easily as if they had met the moon in person. They would never understand that their wives had spent many sunsets watching the world turn just to try and understand that they, too, would someday turn with the world – and in a more intimate way. For their views on life were that of the here and now; the men of the world in that time had to worry about the present, what was visible to their eye there and then. The rare women that could hear the universe spinning were often left to their own devices, alone when they finally went back to the stars they had called family their whole Earth lives. And even then, on the seldom occasion that their men would sit back on the porch they had built with their wives, they still wouldn't understand that their women were those stars, always there to turn with them until they, too, turned.

a hot cup of tea

soothing sores and aches,
a bath to soak in, drain away the pain
teacup sat beside the clawed foot
"peppermint and a special blend"
she smiled as the mistress sipped in the suds
bowed low when she wished to be alone

she returned three hours later
water-soaked floor and bubbles not to be found
the smashed china littering the floor
and a single bay leaf on her chest.

_____ Ω _____
the maiden the mother the crone

i.
the deepest waters run the stillest in their depths
she learned their language at an early age
tossed through waves, bathed in tides
the sun treated her kindly, tickled her skin
freckles doting on her like a grandmother
she entrusted her being to the way of life
and when she spread her arms into the grass
they gave bountifully, singing with her
what you give out will always come back
and she gave with fervor, her love strong
her belief unshakable
she gave her heart and expected nothing back
She took notice.

ii.
clandestine hut, tailored to her soul rather than her hands
bundles of sage dangled where the cats played
a comely face tread the hollow of the room
fire lit, eternally bathing her feet in warmth
newly finished runes etched with care
wooden floor to hold their magic
dried bones and crushed leaves, satchel of sunflowers
in the house of the mother, you are welcome;
the earth is robust here, the waters are demure
the moon gives herself freely, with abandon
while the skies embrace her fiercely
she knows the love of the world, and with it
She grows.

iii.
the waxing moon tugs her
ripening her soul and mind, her body ready to gambol
where she came from is not far from where she went

and her daughters live among the woods,
caretakers of their home
prodigious in their own rights, sailing the love of the maiden
while the crone watches over them

you cannot fish an empty lake, nor sort herbs in a dry garden
there was nothing the sea's moon hadn't taught her;
leathers hung in the corners, waiting for new life
to be gifted to Her, when she needed them

the love she carried was not of small proportions
and it was not a light burden to bear
but the only ones who called it a burden
were the ones who fished the empty lakes,
who farmed the dry gardens.

a promise I will keep

a cult following
built on landfills,
no stars align
under their dying frills.

my voice is MINE
the tales were never yours,
you opened insanity
shut all your doors.

'forgive and forget',
that's what they all say
but my demons remember you—

in fact,
they promise to repay.

──── Ω ────
politics are crossroads

and I am free;

it was a burden to be put down
never will see eye to eye
generational gap? maybe,
informational fuckery? oh yes—

the instance in which a friend
is not a friend, and controls
your friend is sometimes called
peer pressure, while others
call it bullying; and I am not
a teacher, but you were not a
leader, but a follower—

I missed the aspect of a family,
not the daily anxiety
or the treading of eggshells
but it can be imitated,
it can be duplicated —

I do not miss you,
She does not miss him
we are queens without you
and we are, unequivocally
better off without you
and I am free—

_____ Ω _____
change for the—

she treats leaving like a grief she must accept
mourning for menial loss, when no life has been lost
a circumstance, a choice, a little bit of both
the flow won't be stopped;
sure, dampened and maybe sputtering,
but the beams that held up her roof
are no longer there
and she doesn't know what will get her first:

the rain
the snow
the weasel
the melancholy.

Ω
language of the sword

but you only understand the language of the sword
and I learned it through the brutal words you hurled,
a jet stream of lies that led to the slow topple
of a once shining beacon;

but here's a secret from the maw of the forge—
every sword starts with an idea
shaped with the attention and love
of a master, at the request of a heart filled
with justice and thought
and the hindsight wisdom to never trust
the knife that cuts both sides of the lines

so while you stand, I will speak of the sword
and while you berate, I will forge

and when you fall, I will hear it
we will hear it.

_____ Ω _____
dominus tecum

hymns of the faithful, and those with long memories
turn their faces skyward
as the ash of an almost-millennia
touches down in a gentle sorrow

Ave Maria, gratia plena
bless the people who answered the call
risked life and love to save it all
let the church bells ring
as they still stand tall —

the hearts of the world reached out
fingertips on point zero of the french heart
and though we weep alongside you
history will rise like the phoenix,
as history is wont to do —

so keep faith,
hold hope,
dominus tecum

Ω
blood in the water

you couldn't admit you were toxic
tossing bodies like rags,
poisoned the well while preaching with holy water
the price of your ego will pick up the pace
settle itself between your eyes
the target on your back isn't fake
the crossbow in my arms isn't pretend.

the little queen

the light heart of cotton is edged by the strength of leather,
and reinforced with the lash of silk and steel;
velvet and soft, plated under with gold and crimson,
a crest of dignity and loyalty, pride.

her crown is a gift, a statement, bold.
commander of many, a servant to none;
but the gift from a King is no small gesture,
and she wears it with his love, a promise in a royal vesture.

and some claim to know her, while others merely pretend
but her King, oh
he had mapped her every twist, turn, sigh, and bend.
and to her he gave freedom, in the way they both knew,
from their hands rose high, the most viscous of truths.

4.44 am

and all my thoughts are writhing like rapids
the stars hang low in the sky;
if you were a word, I'd give to you this—
you are *komorebi*, the light in my eyes.

and I

and I'm trying to find the words
to tell you what I mean
when I say you're the sun and stars,
you'll never fade away.

and I'm trying to pen the letters
to explain myself tonight
and every time I start a line
you simply fill my sight.

Ω
the quarry

the headlights don't reach the forest
and the fog doesn't touch the sky;

careful where you tread

when the wolf and the maiden are nigh.

Ω
no solicitors

a finger down your jaw,
fighting silence with raw power,
she battles an invisible enemy
with nothing but her voice.

there is conviction and certainty
and devotion
don't misunderstand, but
you won't ever understand.

Ω
it's past tense because it doesn't matter

she couldn't see the abyss through iron, she just wanted to get back home.
shattered faces and slithering tongues, seeing both sides of the world is the curse of a heterochromia heart,
jaded in one eye, crushed in the other; the shield of metal on her forearm more harm than shield,
it's just drowning silently, with a smile, they coaxed, open arms with razorblade embraces,
they named it the call of the void, she remembered
and wondered what it would look like on the other side

we even took the high road

trapped in the grip of a cruel joke
our gods have no reason to be behind this,

and so they will protect us, and challenge
us to become
all the things we never thought we'd be;

please pause.

our hearts need a rest.

─── Ω ───
closet doors

"tell me your confessions, child"—

once upon a time, god reached out for me
but your god isn't mine, Father
and you will call me a betrayer
but my god fills my heart and my body

tender kisses turn to trembling touches
where we began, the cemetery where you prayed
and she pressed me against the willow tree
told me in whispers what the world meant to her
and then told me what I was about to see;

golden hills and brightly lit stars
I had never seen my life flash before my eyes
but she played the scenes in slow motion
like a master pianist
and I was happy to call her a master—

home was a rancher, dust and pastel
sunflowers and stunted bushes, screen door banging in the wind
her windows flung open to let the sweet summer drift in
where she had me beg for her mercy
but I wanted her wrath;

closet door shanked my shoulders but it couldn't hold me hostage
I wrapped my legs around her waist
she was a god, holding up my world
but what happened when atlas let go of the real thing?
she would catch it, of course

spider hands chilled me, then thrilled me
she said I would have a bad reputation
but I had never wanted to be smote so badly
tell me more about why I can't go to church anymore

young god, hold my life above your head
let me kiss up your thighs, stumble into your heaven

don't let me stay human, don't let me drown in the world
I can't believe it, Father, for I did sin
and you let me go, I left the box
mother mary with a grin in her eye
she knew what I was about, virgin was just another name for careful

she left you on my lap to remind me where I came from
the apple of their eye, snake in their ribs
shake the tears from my breast, lick them clean
open my soul and wear me like a halo
walk with me, humanity beneath my feet

write to the devil, tell him we'll be by
and he'll prepare a banquet for the ghosts we chase there
but the only time I feel alive is in the moments you have lost your vision to me;
your aspirations were to let the seven seas crash into me
build an ark and sail us away

two steps ahead, we became a legend and suddenly the tables turned
the bottom of the barrel was your kiss
tender and poisonous
perhaps the father was right, but not about me
bruised egos live in that chapel, don't tame me with your words
kept down from the best things in life because you were too scared
to take what belonged to you, worried you would fall when you tried to fly

and I take it all back to the days in the cemetery
pressed against the willow tree.

kintsugi

when we shatter, as we so often do, the pieces go missing. disguised in the darkness, kept undercover.

we are broken pottery, dusting the floor of the shop, waiting for the inevitable corn broom that will sweep us away into nothingness. but not all that is broken is worth nothing. in loving hands, yours or theirs, searing gold into your scars and sealing your goals in an enlightened way. you return to the world whole, wiser. compassionate for those swept away. use it.

bad moon rising

you said this free-falling feeling
is what it felt like to be lost in the world
and I had always been afraid of heights,
but it had seemed simpler in your eyes;

laying at your feet
I will raise you up like the Sistine
a prime lover, a beautiful misnomer
you never asked for it
but you brought me back to life,
so does that make you the necromancer
to my tired soul?

careening into the chasm of nothing
effervescent lights
imbued with the screams of the damned
and I cannot find my way out of this maze
I'm too old to catch feelings
but this was like a flag in the wind

white flag, catch me—

I took the mantle you left behind
it was all I can see,
once I wrote for myself
but I always try harder when it's for someone else
there is no exception, untold law

drag the breath from my rib cage
and I will paint it gold
a lullaby to be portrayed later,
an award here, a kind word there
oblivious to the fine print
'see me'

Ω
arsonist's lullaby

you must run
as fast as you can
they will catch you
haunt you
deign you immor(t)al
and keep you forever—

tattered swords
bloody rags
rolling of the feet and
the agony of the people
pray you prayed hard enough
every fleeting look
is one more moment
for them
to catch up

hands reaching out to you
don't get lost now
the docks are there
the boat is in sight
you can make it
just jump—

learning to be

listening to the signs and signals around me
is so much harder to do
than it is to ignore them.

it is time, they say.
but what if I don't want it to be time?
I know in my heart of hearts that it rests before me,
one step from the precipice that will allow me to be
f r e e
allow me to start healing—

you are hurting yourself, they say.
well, what if I like the pain?
learning to speak is a struggle,
sharing my heart and hurt is scary
but I am learning to be brave,
acknowledging that I am, perhaps,
worthy.
that I am, perhaps, broken,
but not discarded.

it is okay to strain,
if you remember to grab the hand that reaches out.
it is so hard to remember that, sometimes.
but I think I'm doing it.

leaning into embers

the freight train in the middle of my head
blows the whistle at your stop, every stop
resting witch face,
pressed against the glass
waiting, waiting for what
I do not know.

there is a film, so gaudy and clouded,
enough to see through the illusion
not enough to hold it back
susceptible to the night,
maybe that's why Nyx chose me—
maybe that's why I bleed—

sometimes it is like someone took a knife to the soul
and yes, you cool my desire.
contentment sways her hips between the two—
perhaps we are always meant to be on fire.

almost within view

I can almost see you,
twilight-lit, framed by oaks
tail-end of a wish, your halo
lit like a miracle,
shining like a shield;

I can almost see you,
hidden ripples in the ocean
delving deep for treasure
there is nothing surface about this—
toes dipped, plunged;

I can almost see you,
waist-deep, treading
call of the sea,
always the call of the mountainous sea

a lost bet

that was heavy,
I wasn't quite ready
for the energy that was verbalized
could see it clearly,
hear it significantly,
so nonchalant.
bleed is real,
maybe not into the page right now
or maybe it's a different kind of paper
and we won't regress
we can't afford to—
but I was reminded that
after all that has been dealt
I never should have bet on you.

the girl with crystals in her pockets

rose quartz, amethyst,
plate of obsidian wrapped in my palm
the full moon waged her wars
between the light and dirty
to assist me,
all for me—

it hangs from my neck,
She rests a hand on my shoulder
I would not take Her for granted
ever the glimmering comfort
She Who Listens to Me

prayers written in my book
to tell Her I am grateful
for Her wisdom and Her patience
while I follow the path through the grass

obsidian wrapped in my palm
rose quartz by my heart,
amethyst in my mouth

I will myself to peace.

the strangest plants

the strangest plants
do not grow just with sun and soil.
they teeter on cliffs,
they weather storms
they face mankind

and come out a beautiful
as any rose

symphony

she used to pray to st. jude
loss left her listless
scraped and bruised, oh, st. jude—

and then the cavern collapsed, and
past lives ran by her like music;
she saw his face, this wasn't their first dance
was it?

whisper-silent, gradual introduction,
she felt like a shotgun, pointed the wrong direction
felt more comfortable in chaos—

she cannot keep her words to herself
the roar and rush of the falls that bellowed
inside her, hoarse

tipped out the amphora's contents at her feet
left in the wake of his bruising mouth
no need for gunpowder when he cocked her heart

thinking about this too much,
hearing your voice in her mind
stopping thinking, start *feeling*

learning to rediscover you,
rediscover me,
this isn't reinvention
this is reinvigoration

nervous beginnings,
caught her unawares—
love is chaos, the blasted fool

now nerve endings, rising at words
soft rendering of touch
editing, retouching, but

they have already seen the mistakes
they're corrected together—

it is hard to corral the music
of the heart
when the orchestra changes instruments every day
but the melody holds the same meanings
the conductor still holds the same feelings

_____ Ω _____
I am a gallery

I am a gallery, long floored and wide brimmed
no footsteps from tourists have padded these halls,
signs suggesting an escape from my reality are nonexistent.
these white-washed walls stand at attention
for my eyes only; examining the lives I lived
many moons before.
The doors are barred, blockading the outside world:
these halls will only host echoes and silent smiles,
where my artwork patiently ages...
I must peruse this museum of life alone.

ash, fir, and pine,
framed in symmetrical rows,
molded and carved between my own hands
until I thought them fine for such golden moments.
beneath each story, a silver plaque lays its head,
with names etched into them like quill on parchment.
these were the souls and bright eyes
I once gave legendary status to;
for once upon a time, they were larger than life.

the rogue, brighter than the moon
he dripped in jewels and light, most becomingly
with eyes that always carried a smile, sometimes a little sorrowful
his mouth covered with wine stains I dared not ask about;
what morally lost princess could turn away from him,
he who carved my name into his heart and crown—
yet somehow, through my rosy visions, I never noticed
his backdrop of velvet was already dirty.
a deeper heart would know, and see,
through our sheaves of bandwidth and jungle of cords
that longevity was in the cards, but not eternity;
I did not know how to read them back then.

we rode better roller coasters than Six Flags
swallowed swells and carried waves,
este amor no estaba destinado a ser.
I longed to hold him to me, for his laugh to touch my ears
where were the fates when we needed them most?
our nights were filled with passionate music making
and would wrap the early dawn in perpetual enthusiasm;
we raised each other up, over mountains and canyons—
we did what we were meant to do, and we loved every moment.
we had triumphed where others had fallen,
learning the meaning of trust and hope, even when it was tiring
and loving with every fiber we could muster,
though few others would ever attest to it.
but, like a woolen blanket spread across the rocks
waiting for the sun to burn it dry,
we let the rays soak for too long, hovering on the edge
before ash and fire could be smelt like rain after a hot day
all mountains must eventually crumble,
some into the sea's roiling embrace.
we tumbled into a smoky gap,
with only the twilight to fill the space in our hearts.
an unpredictable future withheld—
perhaps that was what kept us going for so long;
the knowledge of unknowing, looped in mystery ...
but our rope had been cut, shorn like spring sheep
there were too many cards down, too little chips left.
we were a double-edged wound that wouldn't stay shut.
our silence felt like harsh singing in my lungs
like a wet blanket over my mouth.
we were so young, so in love, so helpless;
I felt as if years had fallen on top of me, too heavy.
who said it is better to love and lose
than to love at all?
life always scolded us, warned us it wasn't fair.
I could only shake my head, commit to memory
what my heart did not wish to learn,

and move to the next story in my halls.

the little lion man, sharp and a gutter
who shattered the illusion.
a storyteller that spoke of desert dunes,
wild nights in the field, flames beyond man's reach
uncensored, but not uncouth
it was just what my lackluster fingers needed.
we tread down winding paths unbeknownst to us
finding forks and hidden hollows, dark foliage
and hopeful shrubs.
but the breadcrumb trail did rise,
and clear sea breeze skies once out of the woods.
I did not go wanting when I yearned
to learn something new.
the old and new jumped to life
and we sifted through it all together,
his patience had boundaries, his compassion wrung thin, but
he drew me out like fresh taffy, sinking his teeth in when ready;
my mind's eye took an aerial view of all life,
while the world swirled below like coffee.
with him, suddenly the moon and stars were in reach,
we just needed the keys to the ignition.
but storms did appear, anticipation and doubt
disabled the strength in myself that I once believed in.
I was only human, I cried, I could only go where my dreams went
that was the path I wanted to follow,
no thought of the miles that accompanied them
we did not say goodbye,
he could not stand the word.
I left his side more than once
tried to keep my head from the deep blue.
the pain only grew, vast expanses of blood sinking me
and I hoped, every day, that it would all end
whatever end that may have been.
it would be many moons before those wounds

would stop oozing; or, perhaps, stop gushing.
our story lay scars, one on top of another,
over my most sacred of feelings.
I played them like a projection slide,
and carried on.

the lone ranger, hidden in the woods
bow in hand, wit at the ready—
he was made of fire and lightning,
earthquakes and avalanches;
he would twist others into elaborate dances
with the grin of a wolf on his lips.
he was the yin to my yang,
dark energy to the green light
helen to troy,
he was wicked and true,
unforgiving and nurturing;
he could make a woman melt
with but a mere sentence.
he created laughter and curated frowns
introduced me to cynicism, suspicion
people were not trustworthy,
and heaven help the human who turned on him.
he was not of this world; he did not live in this plane
the water and earth were his home,
living free on the currents that slipped past his dwellings
the sun would beg to chase his heels,
to gambol alongside his daily wander,
he gave and took life away in such simple manners
it was fascinating and terrifying to watch.
we were lost kids,
built in hell and love, burning the countryside together
we lusted for the mountains to be our backyard,
and did not have to tame that quiet beast when we sat side by side
he had a thirst that could not be slaked,

and a mind that could never be still,
conversation would go on forever, intelligent or hearsay
but we did not stop, and we never held back.
fate is cruel, that timeless bitch
his sanity called for a retreat, falling back to his own
I called to him in my dreams, but the response never came
I became a nightmare, walking through my own seven circles;
I had become the sun that begged to chase his heels,
only to be met by the night every day.
I loved him purely, no restraints or knots.
he was wild and polished, and he built me like a bonfire
I will forever dream of a day when perhaps
he will be there again; a different life time, the same soul.

these spiral stairs take me down the lane
spotlights on the good times,
full of raucous laughter and care;
I move past the blank, the filthy: my enemies.
for over the years, strings are cut—
sometimes, torn,
but a puzzle does not cease to be one
when the pieces are no longer together.
I can hear the scorn, feel the heat,
what kind of person sees love, and not hate?
when does the world stop spinning when plunged into night?
you care not how I see the world, light filled and hopeful
love lives on every year, through us all—
a single human cannot live forever and on,
only to see one other entity as clearly as themselves in a mirror.
these are my treasures, my relics – priceless;
tragedies to be learned and mourned upon.
the Threads of Fate once held us fast
tied for all of history to watch over while we sleep.

to him I bring my hopes and dreams, eternal love;
he carries me on wings of patience and luck
the kind girls can only dare to dream of.

his eyes hold the world closely, brighter than the North
he shines through me like a whisper wind on a summer night;
we are the sun and moon, turning to keep the other bright.
we have knotted our strings, entwined beyond the mind
our love holds a sacred, unwritten agreement—
we never leave the other behind.

the doors of my gallery swing closed; oiled hinges make no sound.
the key of my design I leave inside, safe-kept by my wards.
my timeline is not freely given away to man or beast;
I shall carry my memories until I should have long past died.
their strength in time, and their hold on my essence,
those are the things that make a person become who they are.

and in the end,
when the doors shut for the night,
we all dissolve into stars;
I am nothing but a nightlight.

1666

st. peter, arsonist to the center of the universe
london bridges burning through the twilight
while its people fled into the stars
terror in the form of white-hot heat
scorching st. paul's house of rest—
he carried a grudge like no other;

shattered glass litters the cobblestone
while the clock cries into the night
we count the dead, the ones that mattered
keening the lament of the lost
where their bones rest heavy, ashen and dissolved

rest now, london bridges, carry your wards home
through the river waters and to the sea
we may not follow, but our hearts lie with the broken
and we break burnt bread for their parched throats.

Ω
numen of winter

great goddess of the winter
shrouded in the furs of your priestesses
cocooned in the sanctum of your believers;
tendrils of vivid white frame the slopes of your face
delicate and sturdy, one could say
a glance could slay those most worthy
bring a man to his knees
swell a woman's heart—
icy demeanor you have not,
sister to the underworld
but a certain calm that enables the stuttering of bards
and the muteness of the wild
you reign from a lofty perch,
not so insurmountable for mortals
but so much that they must be ready for peril
and are welcomed with open arms
should they conquer the treacherous hills
of Azgaird, home of the winter goddess

samhain

children of the wolves,
long hair tangled in the northern wind
the snow bothers you not,
packed deep into the hillside, it is warm shelter
fire smoke ekes out through the sparse firs
elk in the pit,
and the wounding sound of the wolves' crawls through your bones.
children of the wolves,
brave hearts and iron legs
you live among the kings of the tundra
and wear yourselves proudly.
the furs of the lost grace your shoulders
a reminder of who looks after who,
who oversees the overseers?

___ Ω ___
pirate love song i.

I left my will in an unusual way;
a message in a bottle, set adrift at the beginning of a summer's day.
for my message was not for anyone of my home,
but for those of the same soul, who appreciated the sea spray and foam.
I did not detail gold nor treasure,
but left words of wisdom, and a smile, for good measure.

when Davy Jones comes to my door
and my soul must be sea-bound forever more,
I must bid you caution before adieu,
and I leave you with my words to chew:

not all treasure is gold and silver,
not every mermaid will leave you bewildered
when the music of the sea falls deaf upon your ears,
recall the spray of the water and the blush of the horizon.
when your self has been stolen, and all meaning is black,
take what is yours, steal yourself back.
do not lose your heart, nor lock it away—
one day you'll want it, on a dark and dreary day.
when raising a sword, take consideration of your fate:
why fight, when you can negotiate?
and when your experiences come to pass as memories, remember this forever:
I never regret.
not ever.

pirate love song ii.

she left me with a pistol and a kiss,
her bare ankles still wet with sand
her hat at her side in a trembling hand.
the shouts of her men rose above the gulls
calling for their captain to take the helm;
how did I come to be where I am?

standing on a lonesome beach with naught but
my heart in her hands?

think of me when the tides turn, she would whisper
though her eyes were already on the horizon.
I never wondered where she went,
for she always returned home
following the writing in the sand.

pirate love song iii.

one foot in the water,
dare I race after your retreating back?
how the wind screamed when you bade me farewell
how the rum flowed heavily through your veins.
the face of flames scored my mind, thick in my heart

I will follow to world's end
to the sandy beaches of nowhere
my mettle will be stronger than the sea
launching my prow into the hard waters of the world

no captain will outrace me
no ship will outgun me
no crew will override me
and when the waters come to claim me as their own
Davy Jones will greet me as equal
for none could sway the pirate that you have left in my heart.

_____ Ω _____
pirate love song iv.

the rain shattered any illusions of safety
as we clung to the mast for our lives;
Davy Jones was coming, incensed by his scorned lover
Calypso, goddess of the sea, you have loyalty to none but yourself
or so the legends go;

did you cast him aside, setting him on a path of eternal warfare?
knowing that he would follow your words out of love,
as the stories all go -

or was there a deeper meaning behind it all,
meant for his heart only while you watched him sail,
setting typhoons against his enemies
crewing his ship with the damned, knowing his authority would tame them
and waiting, locket in hand, for your love to return
as sure as the tide turns.

perhaps we judge too soon, scrutinizing the worlds of the otherworldly
comparing them to our own stories and passing sentences
as swiftly as a blade.

_____ Ω _____
as one

we are children of the universe;
brimming with the atoms of the extraordinary
in full flight of endless possibilities
human born, starlit
it matters not the colour of skin
the curve of my hair
the brightness of my eyes—
we are whole, as constant as the sun
as equal as the rain
as vivid as the moon;

we are time and space, and never have we mattered so much
as we have in this moment.
so when you ask me who I am
where I am from
I will simply answer what we are:
I am a child of the universe
I am human
And we are home

_____ Ω _____
it's a rainy day somewhere

lucifer takes rain checks,
plastered against his chest with the promise of just one more time
and he doesn't mind, time is his bedside partner
and he's well acquainted with the bartender's menu;

a dollar left behind, a tip in advance
chips lost to a poker shark who knew you were bleeding,
but emptied his pockets of band aids before he stepped inside;
the newspaper never reports on the losers of a game
but the winner always made headlines;
"Man Found Alive with The Dead"

lucifer's counting down the minutes until your return,
checkbook in hand,
only to see you've run out of time and ink;
the horror you feel as his smile grows wide
eclipses even the dealer's smirk

your chips have landed, fresh into debt
your screams vibrate off the rosewood
as lucifer collects his debts -
so, the moral of the story is this, children:
make sure you don't leave your good pen at home.

atomic cocktail

you're dragging your essence away
crippled teeth, crumbling like radiated bones
gouging and gnawing at the influx of information that is being downloaded:

Please wait while your system is updated...

the edge of noise is enough to penetrate any digital landscape, never mind the godless creatures that perform their tasks monotonously.
you've never seen the outside world, but it must have substance
it must have life, teeming with activity and spontaneity
it must, for you must have a goal

Your system will now restart

your nuclear core is detonated,
t-minus forever until the sun will shine again
you're the atom bomb, baby
your will is not your own, you were never given a heart
allowed only to watch devastation, brief and glorious,
execute your coding,
don't wait, don't hesitate
hit the red button

it all ends here.

———— Ω ————
interlaced fingers

Hell is not always decorated with the fires of sin
it is not always filled with the heat of betrayal;
Hell is violet skies and chrysanthemums blooming in the garden
it is the sounds of crashing waves upon the comely shoreline
and the dalliance of spring and summer in the twilight.

you can feel like dying amidst the happiest moments,
in the most privileged of settings
it is not dictated that you must be an open wound
bleeding at a monsoon
to cry out for help.
the stones are not set to the rhythm of human emotion -
and thus, in that way, we are free.
if the night is filled with day, and only an ephemeral reminder of humanity remains
to keep your strings to this earth attached—

I implore you, reader, to heed these words:

in the plethora of minds that whir billions of seconds an atom,
reach inside for the hope that lives in there.
you may scream, the redolent scent of helplessness in your senses
and if you cannot stretch, if you have become mute

turn towards the light—
no, not the vestigial fragments we call heaven;
the sovereign beginnings that we have all felt, ancestral and in our hearts

the ones who care.

──── Ω ────
ctrl+v

your shady games, two-toned words
they buy you nothing, not even time
wasted oxygen used on the inflamed words of someone
who does not know the definition of passion—

if the whip is cracked by your own personal hell
do not lay the scars on the ones who have moved mountains;
labor is cheap, but loyalty is not
and you're running into debt.

energy must be two-fold; you live in a dog-eat-shit world,
and you've thrown your bone as a favor
but to whom, I wonder?
we consider it a team effort, not a leadership blunder.

demeter

the cracks of the damned used to spark the source
like a candle in the darkness, it would consume and flare
determined to fight the age old good versus evil;

once, I sowed the grains of zeal, to be harvested in your autumn
you'd write notes of pleading existence,
prayers of persistence and salvation,
and I would answer the call, goddess of harvest

but all plants must die,

persephone, daughter of the dead,
queen of the lost
clawing her way to the surface
your abysmal yowling deafening no one any longer

preach your death sentences somewhere empty
feed your bleeding tears to someone thirsty for the password
I was not born under atlas; I cannot shake your unfathomable discourage
the wish of something more is tangible if you are working for it
to be handed it is something no deity can do

and I am so empty.

Ω
hephaestus

the forge lies before me,
and I kneel before its altar, a sacrifice to the craft;
it is an art to become steel, caressed by fire and carved by water
a process I live and die by
a sacred position, to fold steel for the gods
as I have folded for my wife, my people
I shall not abandon them in times of need
and my anvil shall ring with the thunder of war
but in the stillness of the peaceful era,

where does a master crafter turn to?

Ω
glaucus

t'was the hour of rising,
my wife in bed, the babe asleep
and my work had begun before the light had slipped above the horizon.
my nets in hand, spear in another,
calloused as the bark that washed on the gravel
I settled myself into the rhythm of the day;

but I was to be blessed that day, as was the wishes of the gods

the sandy bar of my home away from home
was occupied by an old man, sunk halfway into the edge of the river
harmless and quiet, he appeared no fiend
and as I neared, he beckoned me to him.

'If ye should catch but one more fish than I,
I shall grant you the ability to never lose a catch.'

and lo and behold, he revealed to me his true nature
the patron of my trade, a blessing to those who have good fortune
and so we sat, whiling the day away
what does one say to an immortal?
prod fun all ye want, but we spoke about the weather
and the upcoming spring.
and when the sun began to sink
he counted his basket and I mine
and I was half a head more than him
and smiled and blessed me, and wished me a fair evening
and to this day I have not seen him again,
but we have never gone hungry since.

———— Ω ————
her aesthetic

she watched her sashay into the deep
dark waves lapping her calves like hungry cats

mentioned something about an aesthetic
but that sounded like a kind of alcohol to me

maybe it was hers

graying skies blotted with darker concerns
and the gulls were screaming about it
like damn cheerleaders from the bleachers,
trying to convince you that you're winning

she said she wasn't

braids wrapped into buns, cat-eyed sunglasses on
an arrow tattooed into her back
always bragging that someone would put one there eventually
so why not beat them to it?

and one day, the waves took her into its arms
and never let go.

I looked for her arrow every day
but even the gulls knew it was gone for good.

Ω
completely unsettled

when the angel falls, and the catcher is away
how does one deal with the feeling of loss, though there is
(thank you gods) none?

I do not pray, but I prayed today
I do not believe in Him, but I prayed to my own today
I will never give up, never

but oh, what a wound.

and whatever the reason, myself or something more
it will never be as bad as
if I lost you.

the shield

I do not fit the box we are given when we are growing up
it has been beaten from the inside far too much
the crumbling cardboard doesn't emulate the woman
that has evolved from my skin.

and there's something in the way my hand rests on your arm
that makes you more aware of the white noise in your ears
and I have never been one to sit on the sidelines
heroes must rise to the top with their own two feet,

you shook yourself off, the dust settled around your boots
and you gave back that number you were holding
started your own answers
began your own line

I can't feel anything from the vibrations
but I don't need anything but the honor and the glory
we bleed promise, we exhale legendary
and if we cannot succeed triumphantly,

we will watch over you.

Ω
the glaive

the glaive in the sky
wide as a gyrfalcon
illuminate your message
spread your words through the shadows
and listen carefully for your answer
upon sweet fingertips and soft skin.

─── Ω ───
soft serve soul

soft serve soul
tangy setting sun
dipped in starlight chocolate
waffle blanket
a beautiful addition to the world

the miner left the cage open again

a husk
cyanide citrus seed, emptied into my eyes
I'll be spitting poison for weeks, goddamn you Revered Mother
I have walked another circle in the crop
tide over a beggar for the night
sipped black honey still the stars were in my mouth
and not my heart
super nova-caine indentured throughout my jaw
it's how I live my life until I find the right wrench
to pry my thoughts apart, care less about love and more about life
a paperback novel on my coffee table
my name screamed all over it
and still the siesta careened down
passing the canary in the tunnel
if there is one thing I have learned,
it is to never trust a miner.

Ω
nothing personal

I used to believe in superheroes,
living in the aftermath of their wake
zero hour, saved the day once more—

I don't believe in that anymore.

I put my stock in the human heart
in the mind
my shangri la is inside the emotions
one feels when you stand for something
greater than yourself

justice is not just for the warriors

and I can feel the whispers behind the screens
the goings-on of the powers that think they be
and I admit
the first mistake I made was putting my trust
in the ones with a decorated title
and I forgot myself — accolades aren't indicative of intention

the wind blows from all directions,
even if the compass points north
and I had let myself drift into open sea
uncharted waters can be learned
if your first mate is sea (trust) worthy
so, what do you do when the mast is rerouted
sailing for certain mutiny?
well, you drown the crew in the rain
of course.

―――― Ω ――――

his sympathies lie with me

listen closely, child, for I have a tale to tell
and it all started with a babe, and the depths of hell—

the labyrinthine path to nowhere was surreptitious
the subtle hint of rot imbued in my clothes;
lantern flickering like a candle in a squall,
a dalliance in the shadows of his cloak

fate's strands lay like broken dolls across railings
ephemeral hearts buried in stalagmites,
and where the sky used to be a village
now only lay the sins of the dying sun,
where the ones who couldn't survive were skewered

we met by the Central Well,
howling Nimrod a searing cacophony to my ears
a better person would not question the fallen angel but,
how does one not see past his evanescent mask?
I was a mellifluous prayer in his eyes, and I braced myself
my fate in the ninth circle to be proclaimed from his dark lips

you are ready was his observation, eloquent and yet astonished
how many opulent evenings had we spent together?
my people would see me hang, if they knew
and still he saw me as a redolent escape
and if I said yes, it was the beginning of the end, but
also the true beginning...

and if ready means being alive for seventeen years,
then I am.

Dis was more than prepared, and careful Antaeus allowed me to gaze
into the afterlife of my choosing:

a frozen landscape, eternal screaming, the throne of the damned:

where else should a witch lover reside, if not at her God's side?
don't tell Judas that—

his bargain was burned into my skin, as if afraid I would retract
and I wondered once more why he was choosing me, lonely and lovely—
he brought me to his rooms, finer than Dis should receive
his susurrous promises gracing my tongue
perhaps God turned a blind eye to his favourite on this matter...

we parted at the surface, no trace of mischief in his gaze
all pretense of power simmering away
he knew we were the panoply of existence
and I reveled in this, quietly
his ebullience at my eventual return was endearing;
see you soon

my child, you have wondered where we wander
why we smile during the thunderstorms
and I tell you now—
there is mercy in the devil,
it lives within you
and has rooted in my heart.

so when we return to that rock face
carved elegantly with malediction
remember it is a warning to the ones behind us
and a welcome from the ones before us—

today, I return home to my God,
today, you learn of your roots.

──── Ω ────
orphaned time

in the corners of the stars,
a timeline all its own
your name is not hidden but celebrated -
from the darkest galaxies you could find
to the brightest smiles of students
you were the Doctor:
you were the Doctor on the day it wasn't possible to get it right,
and it cost you more than your humanity
and all of your memories.
overflowing with the burden of pain and mercy—
to watch your world ignite,
to never feel whole again
and you counted those numbers for centuries.
yet, a choice was made ready:
a spark of magic was still left,
coalescing in your heart—

the deepest knowledge of magic's roots
lay in the great abyss of your mind
terrible and wondrous
safekeeping as much as you could
guiding the young to the gateways of their path
magnificent, even in the face of death incarnate—

I have heard tell that the TARDIS brings hope
its coughing and whirring likened to oxygen and a heartbeat
wherever it may come;
the wand chooses the wizard
and you were keeper of them all;
you were built in the fires of war,
tested by the mettle of humanity
welded by the iron that held our worlds together
now free flowing through a carven mold

do not forget us!

for we could never forget you—
Ollivander, keeper of secrets and gifter of experience
you were the first light of home
when we but tapped that brick in the wall,
found by counting three up and two across, thrice

War Doctor, survivor in peace and unsettled in heart
but lo, your hearts were changed when you looked upon yourself
and remembered why you were here,
why you are the healer and the storm
why your name was a pillar in the galaxies to come.

great men are forged in fire.
and it was our privilege to light the flame.
you were the beacon that led us all on a journey,
and I could never lose your memory of stalwart strength—

may the magic never die from your name
your wisdom be entombed in the archives of our hearts
and Gallifrey be the light in your stars above.

written in memory of Sir John Hurt.

with flowers in your hair

sunflower girl, petals in your hair,
you are always found in the long grasses
waving in the summer air.
dreamcatcher above your bed, you save the nightmares
in hopes that you can tame them,
dispel fear as fiercely as a lion on game.
hemp belt hung with jade miniatures
the eagle, the bear, the stag
your heart drifting on the hazy days
and eagerly captivating the youngsters by campfire nights
with tales of the moon and the hare,
the salmon and the bear
the raven and the mountain
and when the sun crests the snowy peaks
and the smoke curls under the peregrine's wings
you'll disappear into the long grasses
waving in the summer air.

———— Ω ————
whittle me of willow wood

whittle me in willow wood,
spider silk strands as strong as an oak
soft as the breeze
I offer you my undying strength for your body, mind
spirit.
the heaviest of burdens would lay upon my shoulders
gladly
if to give you a season of recuperation.
my strings hum sweetly, weaving stories of mountains bold
and warriors tall, each uniquely a war-drum
ready to induce the boiling that all battle brings to its halls.

I write, the clack of the keys 'neath my hands break silence
every instant a new story stirs my mind. steam rises
from my mug, stems of lavender decorating the ash wood
while the lives of new people flow through my fingertips
a heartbreak, a mistake, something re-evaluates
time to take a break;

eased into the sweltering heat of the desert,
one cannot help but wear white
in hopes that the waves will carry you away with them
I have always loved the heat,
passion-driven, exhalation of dirty deeds done
in the name of the Redeemer
but the true wonders of this place
reside above; for when you look up
all the heavens deem you worthy
and spill down your cheeks in a newly created Via Lactea.

――― Ω ―――
delve deeper into the plot, with caramel on the side

she need not shout to the heavens,
for she resides in them
she does not look to the stars
for they are in her eyes;
waves of soft change shift her constant,
and she is not of this flow, instead a steady stream of consciousness
deep within her fragile skin, a jewel sacred to none but her
a well of knowledge, a pool of peace
and the fragrance of hazelnut wafts the breeze
like amber silk in the solstice winds.

there is no inspiration like that of mankind
for each footstep is a story that marks the beginning of a new start
destructive and beautiful, every movement worth spinning a tapestry;
the constellations a charter to your home
a ferry waiting to take you to the future
sweet like much-deserved dessert, savored twice and more plentiful
and what is this all about if not a charmed life,
as long as you believe in the divination of your soul
as long as you believe in the ecstasy of your life?

fairy dust through the foggy woods

the tipping of water-soaked trees left me with naught but cool trickles
left to remind me of the ebullience of the rivers that course beside us
quiet respite, most treasured peace
in the tomorrow's day, it is fleeting, only a second to experience;
but here, we are stopped and allowed to reflect
imbuing the grace and leisure that only the fog can give us.
a lagniappe to oneself, is friendship,
mellifluous is the whir of magic
sprinkled in the deep woods; ye who take a spring at chance
would be greeted wholeheartedly—
trail-blaze through the mists with me,
for I could not forget you
as you could not forget yourself.

of ravens and classics

hither towards immortality,
ye who live onwards in the light
what sanctions did the angels give ye, dead in the mountains
when the fires did fall upon the queen's ankles?
ah, to dream in the kaleidoscope of Shakespeare,
he who dared to break the lines of conformity
presented the world with a modern day
love of life;
we sing of namaste
but do you not remember the savanna of trials?
and we roared like disney's prince when we triumphed
over that which we thought was impossible;
because the strength in which our heart's reside
comes from not above, but deep within,
when the meteor showers crowd out the sun
imminent life is sitting on the cusp of our lifespans—
normandy, my love, we would captain thee beautifully
sail the endless confines of the black seas
like the shepherd that manned humanity's course;
a new tale waiting to be spun,
another calibration to be corrected—
a new shrine to erect,
more rum to drink.

Ω
old soul, young at heart

melting macchiato, creamy and soothing
while the fall of autumn turns the windows from hazy dust
to sparkling remembrance
and I recall why the heart is always the first to jump;
a sloping shoulder, mis-covered by a favourite sweater
what is there to hide, when I have shown my true colours
in every care I have gifted to those that are family
but cannot recall my name.
incense that smells like our old treehouse burns deep
calling to mind all the old wars
healing the broken,
helping the forsaken,
easing the long gone.
we played doctor when we were younger,
never thinking one day I would truly set that broken arm of yours
never thinking one day you would be sealing my heart up again.

we played games long into the evening,
sometimes you'd even let me win backgammon
you didn't know I let you win
and it is those times that I would sift through my memories for
because the tears of life
are often stronger than
the laughter of death.

Ω
so what about magical space aliens

what is life without a little mystery?
the trickle of memories I cannot cling to
glide on the edges of my mind, lost to my eyes
I reminisce about my home,
that I have never known,
and weep for the love I have lost
that I cannot remember.
where have you gone, precious existence!
we should be swapping old tales
in the fields of gold, basking under a pastel sky
never have I felt so alone and together at once,
it is wrong to assume I am but one being
but is it to tell me I am wrong?
our journeys are vastly unalike
and yet here we are, walking the roads of your youth
not knowing if those are the skies of mine.

but what is life without a little mystery,
and I am trying to find the memories of myself
one dusty book at a time.

a serendipitous moment, friend

unexpected fortune,
equally as joyous and profoundly favoured
as the lucky cat that sits in the window sill of your favourite antique shop.
wound upon itself is the fabled red string of fate
a flask of wine to settle us in the journey
you never would have guessed that we had never met,
with the stories that were told on the gondola,
lotus and firefly pausing to listen as we gambled on stars
wrote about the crane,
whistled with the koi.
a thousand countless moments of inspiration
are suspended in the paper lanterns above the river
caught by the gods that are sent these tributes of the heart
for what better gift is that than a piece of yourself?
sound off on the mountain slopes,
hear our voices sing high
like the maidens in the falls who call to the summer
an elegant duo, a mingled pair
the zither played from afar, and the sun sets its golden rays
onto the mercury floor, reflecting the strokes of the day,
never forgetting the journey had begun seasons ago
on an unexpected fortune.

always a plot twist, but never when you intend it

the best cushions
are often found in the arms of a friend
the longest nights
turn up in extended stories, rambling codes
spiraling plots and twisting adventures
the wash of energy that is exuded is cleansing
is comforting;
where the wind blows, we too shall be found
for the teacher always learns from the students
more than they would ever admit;
books became our fuel, the galactic unknown is our bond
treading eons upon eras of burning stars
billions of miles away
and yet our hemp rope holds yet
and we do not waver, we stand for much more than just
a simple code, a fleeting feeling,
a codex in the dark.

―――― Ω ――――
through the rich forest

fairy-tale'd chains of marigolds
embroidering the beauty of brooks
bubbling and giggling radiantly
pale gold skin on a delicate frame,
with untamed locks the colour of sand dunes in the south-east
that peeked through the trunks of oaks
like a cradle of light;
whimsical dancing, contemporary and graceful
while the deer admired, the fox glowed
each having been gifted the healing touch of her hands
on a long winter's night;
the grass is certainly only greener where you spread your magic
rolling hills of sempiternal life grew beneath her feet
redolent roses and daisies marking her slumber
when the autumn tongues sweep their way through the branches
and she will awake again in the snowfall
when her touch is needed, once more.

——— Ω ———
you need not a shape to leave an impression

do not fear benevolence,
she is kind and warm, mother to us all
harbinger of our wisdom;
born in a place of hell
she grew to higher spaces
than those musty niches,
carrying those with her that needed to remember
that elixirs only carry so much hope
until you must search inside yourself, hard
she will be by your side,
tarry not in the swell of the uneven
she will be your light in the mundane
until you cast your own glow
deep into the spiraling night.

―――― Ω ――――
galactic endeavors, always a touch away

scholastic creature, golden frames on your nose
you reach for the heavens, not knowing what they are
but understanding they are a part of you
as much as you are a part of them.
you treat the quiet as an opportune moment
to absorb the infinite knowledge of the universe
not one to squander the resources so willingly bestowed
from such an impartial source.
observing the sigma octantis through your crystal lens
sighing over the never-changing stillness of life
residing billions of miles away,
and all the while appreciating that you, yourself
every spark you have given off
has come from one of those distant ancestors
and perhaps, one day,
another will look upon the stars as you do now
and realize you birthed them with your spark, too.

Ω
thou art the druid queen

druid queen, silver in your hair
among the texts of your people, you while away your ancient days
each new parchment piece another scale on your magnificent steed;
high are the halls you have built for your people
gifted were you when the people raised you up
for even the creatures of your land paid respect to your wisdom;
mighty stag, king of the forest, begat your crown of bone and velvet
stretching to the tree tops like spires,
noble eagle, a feathered cape to alight your shoulders in the winter's cold
gold and amber threaded like the stones of the dwarves
honourable wolf, an exquisite pelt to wrap toes and fingers in alike,
both courageous and familial feelings coursing through them

in your people, you have inspired the best of their hearts
breeding love, promoting a body of prestige in virtues and health
and to you, they are your family
to them, you are their salvation.

Ω
a gift you are bored with

I cannot understand when a human tells me
they cannot appreciate the beauty before them
if they have seen it more than once—

mother nature is a gift,
the mountains and the plains,
the scrubby grass and the lush greens
it changes and yet is the same,
ever growing and yet eternal

perhaps I am too ensconced in the beauty
that I live in
or maybe I am just lucky, and I forget this
but to feel as if your home is nothing more than fodder

I cannot relate, and I cannot explain
and I am so sorry.

──── Ω ────
she was careful wish her wishes

She twisted and twirled down the cobblestone road, a basket of roses slung over her arm and a grin on her face. Twin braids sailed in the air, and her sky-blue dress ruffled with every step she took. She whistled a tune few knew, and gave flowers to old folks and beggars as she skipped by. Their reactions were always the same: *Bless you, child! You've made me smile, thank you!* She liked to see them smile, and she considered it her duty to give people a moment of sunshine in their day. Even roses wilted eventually, but not all memories do.

One day a young man stopped before her, ego and pride personified.

"Miss, I do believe you should give me a rose, as a token of your affection."

The young lady cocked her head. "But sir, I don't even know you. You wouldn't instigate an argument with a lady, would you?"

He puffed himself up, his hands jammed into his pockets. "Do you not know who I am? Why, I could make all your dreams come true, with just the flick of my wrist. I could make nations bow before your feet! You'd wear sable and leather for as long as you wished to, and there would be no finer woman."

She thought about it for a moment. "Any wish I could want, you say?"

He nodded, looking pleased with himself. "Anything you desire."

The young lady took a rose from her basket, kissed the top of it, and handed it to him. "Here you are, sir. I wish you'd keep me happy!"

He took it in one motion, triumph and eagerness on his face. "You won't regret pledging yourself to me, madam!" She only smiled at him, and he escorted her to his estate, where they married immediately.

True to his word, she lived in the lap of luxury for many years, as he was a great investor and rarely gambled with his money. One day, many years later, the young lady had grown into a lovely woman, still in her sables and leathers. As she sat by her bedroom window, she caught sight of her husband walking down the same road they had met on, and he stopped a girl carrying a basket of bread. She decided to get closer and listen in on them, and she heard him telling the young girl the same things he had said to her. She turned back to the house when the girl gave him the whole basket of bread, eyes shining with promise.

When he returned home, with the girl in tow, he introduced her to his wife as the new maid. Seeing the shock in her eyes, she greeted her warmly and told her she would take care of everything, and not to worry. Once alone, she told her story and who she was. Through her shock, the two women began plotting their revenge together, becoming fast friends.

One evening, the two women came upon the young man, now much older and powerful. He was arm in arm with two wenches, and was drunker than you could imagine. They stopped before him, and his wife smiled sweetly at the trio, the maid behind her with a basket of roses and bread.

"Husband of mine, I thought you said any wish I wanted would be granted!"

The old man laughed, stumbling against the girls, and shook his head. "I offered you wealth, not love. You are dressing in the windows, my dear, and so is your maid. Money can buy happiness!"

Still smiling, she nodded sagely as the maid stepped forward. She took a loaf of bread from the basket and handed it to her husband. "We understand. Will you at least let us feed you? The three of you look famished."

They took the bread and broke it into three, and upon eating it, the wenches dropped to the ground, eyes rolling into the backs of their heads. The old man screamed as his skin began to turn black.

"What have you done to me, you wretched bitch!"

The maid smiled as he writhed in pain, and she stepped before him. "Don't you know not to make deals with the devil, sir?"
The young man watched in horror as the women changed into succubae. They knelt by his side, the lane peculiarly empty, and he realized he was going to pay for his treachery.

"You were doing so well, and then you had to go and break our little hearts with your ego and conniving. And my poor friend here, you promised her the world and went back on your word in the same day! Shame on you for hunting down women like we're some kind of play thing."

The maid kissed his cheek, her horns tipping against his temple. "I was so looking forward to being a pampered wife, too."
She picked a rose from the basket and looked at her older friend, who nodded with a smile. She kissed the top of it and pressed it against his lips. He gasped in horror, then shriveled into a husk the next moment. His soul had been reclaimed by the devil himself.

Changing back to their human forms, they dusted themselves off and left the man in the road, walking arm in arm back to the estate. The town found him the next day, and chalked it up to poison of some kind. A small funeral was held for him, but no one missed him in lieu of his beautiful and generous wife, whose handmaid would visit the townsfolk and brightened up a room just by being in it. The women gave to the needy and beggars using the estate funds, and they never spared alms when asked. And every holiday season, they would hold a lively feast for everyone, wishing them all the best in the new year. The old man's memory was dust.

His soul, however, was another matter. He sat in hell with the devil, shouting his guilt and pleading mercy whilst the devil listened, hand on his cheek like a patient mother.

"They tricked me! How could I know they were your wives!"

"You shouldn't have been an arse to begin with, why should that make any difference? You don't get to choose who you can be nice to — people of all walks of life deserve to be treated with kindness, even myself. My wives are taking that well in stride using your wealth, and yet no one has any memory of you because of their kindness."

The old man screamed in denial, refusing to be out-bested by women, nevermind strong women. The devil sighed, and walked away, leaving him to his self-inflicted pan.

His wives spent many long years in that town, aging themselves with magic until it was appropriate to fake their deaths and move on. The town erected a small monument to the young women for the goodness they had spread among them all, while they honored the old man through terrible tavern songs. Eventually, even his grave was forgotten, and creeping vines covered his name for eternity, while the devil enjoyed having a new human pet to add to his collection. His wives moved across the country, looking for more men and women that were holding down a community, and tearing them down.

―――― Ω ――――
bad wolf bay

Like fire and ice. I feel every heartbeat that pulses through that galaxy in your veins, the super novae and red dwarfs and asteroid fields and diamond planets that crisscross the expanse of stars that have formed your person. Ground shattering revelations make me quake in delight, lighting up the night sky in my eyes. The shade of blue that flashes through my memory, and all those times you didn't say what I wanted you to say but I told myself that you said it through your actions, every time you took my hand.

And there we stood, a lifetime stretching between us, but a brush of fingertips away on a lonesome splash of wet sand, the waves rolling in like a sigh from the beginning of time. I felt my heart aching and burning up like the sun, my whole being longing to fly to you, but you were just energy — a moment in between two worlds that let me tell you I love you. I never wanted you to be alone. I wanted to live out my short life beside your everlasting self, consumed by nothing but my one desire to be your companion for as long as I lived. I never told you, throughout the dangers and perils, the tears and the travel, the laughter and the memories. I had wanted so badly to hear you, the man who traveled far and wide, the god who lived within time itself, the only person to have seen what I had saw every time I stepped outside those doors with your hand in mine — I wanted to hear you say that I was too right to love you, that I'd be daft if I didn't, and most of all I wanted to hear you tell me you loved me back. All those lifetimes, all those people, all those adventures — and you loved me.

And now here I am, light years away, and your name on my lips. And I still love you, 'til time takes me back for itself.

ACKNOWLEDGEMENT

To Ian and Kuro: The countless hours of reading, writing, collaborations, struggling over words (and the lack thereof sometimes), of the many typos, wild prompts, the longing for more time, and the need for more inspiration that sometimes resulted in doodles and laughter that hurts so good. Thank you for being two of the best friends a woman could ever ask for, after all these years.

To Mellie: My sister in the Craft, writing partner extraordinare, and the greatest woman I've ever had the pleasure of calling best friend. As many times as we have beaten our heads against words, they always seem to fall into place very neatly when we work together, and if that isn't our gods favouring us, I don't what is. *Carpe noctem.*

To the new humans I've met in the fine year of 2022, I'm so grateful for your friendship. All of you have, in some way, contributed to this book, and I am grateful for it.

ABOUT THE AUTHOR

Seren J.h. Wolfe

An award-winning poetess, an author, and visual artist, Seren lives with her incredibly talented husband of six years in beautiful British Columbia.

She has been writing for nearly twenty years, mostly focusing on fiction and poetry. Her favourite things to write about are the occult, religious vibes, royalty, romance, fantasy-adventure, science fiction, women, and death.

Manufactured by Amazon.ca
Acheson, AB